Dedication

To God's faithful servants who have gone before us, both living and in Glory. As one of my colleagues has said: "We stand on giants' shoulders."

** Patrick McElligott: "On Giants' Shoulders" - see book list on p. 96*

above: the Bulstrode Beauty Walk in May

below: a light on a hill - Bulstrode Verandah, with a so-called "supermoon," October 2015 *photo: Anthony Lau*

To Everything a Season — Ecclesiastes 3:1-11

To everything there is a season,
A time for every purpose under heaven:
A time to be born, and a time to die;
A time to plant,
and a time to pluck what is planted;
A time to kill, and a time to heal;
A time to break down, and a time to build up;
A time to weep, and a time to laugh;
A time to mourn, and a time to dance;
A time to cast away stones,
and a time to gather stones;
A time to embrace,
and a time to refrain from embracing;
A time to gain, and a time to lose;
A time to keep, and a time to throw away;
A time to mend, and a time to sew;
A time to keep silence, and a time to speak;
A time to love, and a time to hate;
A time of war, and a time of peace.
What profit has the worker from that
in which he labours?
I have seen the God-given task with which
the sons of men are to be occupied.
He has made everything beautiful in its time.
Also He has put eternity in their hearts,
except that no one can find out the work
that God does from beginning to end.

Never was a truer word spoken! In the physical sense all things are born and all things die. In the realms of Christian work too, dreams and visions are birthed; but the time may come for them to be put to sleep, and for a new vision to take their place.

In WEC's season at Bulstrode there have been times of weeping and times of laughter. Loved ones have passed away and hardships been endured, while countless moments of joy and blessing have also been experienced.

Moving house (and moving out of Bulstrode is one enormous house-move) involves many decisions... what do we keep and what do we throw away? Spiritual growth too requires key moments of choice... "...let us throw off everything that hinders..." *(Hebrews 12:1)*

"We do not wage war as the world does...for our struggle is not against flesh and blood, but against...the powers of this dark world and against the spiritual forces of evil in the heavenly realms." *(1 Corinthians 10:13, Ephesians 6:12)* The weapons we fight with are the Word of God and prayer.

He has made...
"In the beginning God created the heavens and earth" *(Genesis 1:1)*
everything...
"...without Him nothing was made that has been made" *(John 1:3)*
beautiful in its time...
"God saw all that He had made and it was very good" *(Genesis 1:31)*

photo: Eleanor Harvey

WEC International
Bulstrode
Oxford Road
Gerrards Cross
Bucks SL9 8SZ

Dear Reader,

Going...going...gone are the days when I could welcome you in person to Bulstrode through the old, familiar wooden doors and into the lofty surroundings of the Atrium. Instead, I would like to invite you to share with me the story of WEC at Bulstrode through the pages of this book, "To Everything A Season."

Come on in and share the experiences of people who have lived and worked here, read descriptions of the ministries that have operated here and enjoy the numerous photos which evoke the beauty and blessing of the place.

Naturally there's a tinge of sadness as WEC UK moves on to a new era based elsewhere, but my hope and prayer is that this multi-faceted story brings good memories to some, a challenge to others and encouragement to all.

God has done so much in and through the lives of those who have passed through these doors. This book is an attempt to capture something of the "season" when Bulstrode was WEC's temporary home.

Paul M Harvey

Spring 2016

CONTENTS CONTENTS CONTENTS

CONTENTS CONTENTS CONTENTS

GLOSSARY

Every organisation has its own jargon, so this glossary is included to help "non-WECers" (as well as WECers who have forgotten) understand what we are talking about when we use terms like "CO," "IO" and "Volly Helpers."

accepted	*term used when someone joins WEC full time ("commissioning" is used now)*
Betel	*Church-planting movement among addicts (Betel = Bethel or House of God)*
BCS	*Bourofaye Christian School, a WEC MK school in Senegal*
Beauty Walk, the	*circular walk in the Bulstrode gardens*
Boutique, the	*Bulstrode's second-hand clothes store*
Candidate	*applicant to WEC in the orientation phase*
Chapel	*large room used for meetings; also refers to the half hour worship and devotion time each weekday morning*
CO, COC, CC	*Candidate Orientation/Course*
CT Studd	*founder of WEC*
Extension Ministries	*a WEC department for engaging with churches and the public - superseded by the Network Dept and Mobilising Team*
field	*or "branch" - place of service*
furlough	*time at home off the field*
Intercon	*International Conference for WEC leaders*
IO	*International Office*
IRO	*International Research Office*
IS	*International Secretary (latterly changed to Director or Leadership Team)*
Keep, the	*the castellated folly, pigeon tower*
Lime Walk, the Lime Avenue, the	*grand avenue of lime trees in the garden*
MK	*missionary kid, offspring of missionaries*
Long Water, the	*the elongated lake at top of Beauty Walk*
OW	*Operation World*
Press Yard, the	*area where WEC Press used to be*
reaching the unreached	*communicating the good news of Jesus Christ with peoples who have not heard it*
Reception	*Bulstrode's welcome desk*
RUN	*Reaching the Unreached Now*
STEP	*Strategy to Every People programme*
tithe	*the practice of giving 10% to God's work*
Unimatco	*see article on p. 53*
unreached peoples	*missionary term for people groups that have not yet heard the gospel of Jesus*
Volly Helper, Volly, Vollies	*young volunteers who work at Bulstrode in return for board, lodging and English*
WEC	*Worldwide Evangelisation for Christ (the "C" formerly stood for Crusade)*
WECer	*a member of WEC*

ACKNOWLEDGEMENTS

Cover design & production	Brian Cross
Editing & layout	Paul Harvey
Photographs	Colour photos: by Paul Harvey unless otherwise stated Black and white photos: from WEC archives unless otherwise stated
Special thanks to...	All article contributors, Brian Cross, Andrew Bowker and WEC Publications, Rose Harvey, John Gravett, Shiela Gravett, Linda Sullivan, Rebecca de Vos, Carolyn Davey, Gweno Hugh-Jones, Barbara Birch, Janet Stewart, Wayne Robinson, John Bagg
And to the following for photographs...	Anthony Lau, WEC Press, WEC Archives, Dave Northcote, Iain Fairweather, Savills, Jean Goodenough, Sheena Wardrope, David Burnett, WEC Youth, Hwa Jeong, Joyce Gledhill, David Paul, Richard Davey, Eleanor Harvey, Sam Harvey, Rose Harvey, Wendy Baldwin, Heather Donnelly, Anthony Franks, Crissy Brinker, Chrissie Brown, Rosamund Ramsden, Adam Lowe, Francis Blackmore, Rahel Grossmann, Jessica Mezquita, Brian Cross, C & K Witty, T and J Kallmier, Jackie Rowe, Unimatco

Yellow Iris on Bulstrode Pond

Some photographs in this book and other resources are available at www.bible100s.co.uk

INTRODUCTION

About WEC — 3 Aims, 4 Pillars

Many of you reading this will be WECers, but for those who are not, here's a brief snapshot. WEC *(Worldwide Evangelisation for Christ)* is an international Mission Agency of about 1,800 workers in approximately 70 fields, or branches. The three main aims or objectives of WEC are:

1. **Pioneer Evangelism** - taking the gospel of Jesus Christ to people who have not heard it.

2. **Church Planting** - forming communities of Christian disciples.

3. **Mission Mobilisation** - inspiring and training disciples of Jesus to take the message of Jesus to others, often crossing cultural boundaries while doing so.

But WEC is more than an organisation. It is also a family - a family of ordinary people whose ethos is summed up in 4 pillars:

*they live by **faith**

*they are willing to face **sacrifice** when necessary to follow their God-given calling

*they practise **holiness** with the help of the Holy Spirit

*they enjoy **fellowship** with one another across the miles and through the generations

About Bulstrode — Four H's

History - Bulstrode has a fascinating past, the highlights of which are described in the timeline which follows on the next page.

House - The present house dates from the 1860s, while the Keep is a solitary reminder of a previous mansion on the site.

Horticulture - The gardens are magnificent at any time of year and the Beauty Walk contains spectacular rare trees from far-flung parts of the globe. Many are illustrated in this book.

Heritage - There has been a vibrant Christian witness at Bulstrode for at least 6 decades (with WEC and the Bruderhof before them). This book tells the living story of that witness.

Year of Jubilee — The 49th and 50th Years

1967 to 2016 covers a period of 49 years. A random number, one might think...for it just happened to be in the year 2016 that the WEC UK Fellowship decided to take stock of its role in society and relocate its Headquarters out of Bulstrode, spreading its staff members more widely around the country. However, the period of 49 years is not without Biblical precedence:

"Count off seven sabbaths of years - seven times seven years - so that the seven sabbaths of years amount to a period of forty-nine years. Then have the trumpet sounded everywhere ...Consecrate the fiftieth year and proclaim liberty throughout the land to all its inhabitants. The fiftieth year shall be a jubilee for you." (Leviticus 25:8ff)

Without over-stretching the symbolism of this comparison, I believe we can draw encouragement at this momentous time in WEC's journey of faith, by considering the theological heart of the Biblical jubilee. What did the jubliee mean to God's people?

1. The seventh sabbath in the 49th year was to be a time of re-evaluation, of putting things in order, of remembering again that the land and everything else belonged not to them, but to God.

2. The sounding of the trumpet was a clarion call to gather together before the Lord, a rallying cry to action, a resounding symbol of celebration.

3. The 50th year, the actual jubilee, was to be a time of thanksgiving, of starting afresh and of renewed blessing from the Lord.

WEC relocates from Bulstrode after 49 years, closing a fruitful and blessed period in our history. As we step into a new era for WEC in the "jubilee year," we can step out in faith, knowing that our God is with us, He is behind us and He goes before us.

Bulstrode Park Timeline

showing key dates below and occupancy at right

Year

1600

The first mention of the name Bulstrode comes from the time of William the Conqueror, when an Anglo-Saxon overlord called Shobbington defended his land against the new Norman King. One story relates that he went to London to negotiate terms (a promise of allegiance to the King in return for his land) riding on a bull. After such a memorable trip astride a bull, he naturally acquired the name Shobbington-*Bulstrode*, and soon the Shobbington part was dropped to leave simply Bulstrode. This story, along with other information below, has been gleaned from Audrey Baker's *History of Bulstrode* and other sources. *(see p. 96)*

1650

1645	Bulstrode family sell Bulstrode Park to Thomas Gomer for £1,800
1652	Thomas Gomer sells to Ambrose Bennett for £2,850
1675	Ambrose Bennet dies. Judge George Jeffreys buys Hedgerley Bulstrode and rebuilds
1676	Jeffreys also buys Temple Bulstrode - King Charles II dines with Jeffreys at Bulstrode
1689	King James II flees the country - disgraced Judge Jeffreys dies in the Tower

1700

c.1700	Jeffrey's family sell to Hans William Bendinck - a favourite of the new King William of Orange, who makes him Earl of Portland in gratitude for his support
1709	Bendinck, Earl of Portland, dies - his son Henry inherits
c.1710	Henry made 1st Duke of Portland by Queen Anne - the Queen visits Bulstrode
1730s	His son William and his wife, Lady Margaret Cavendish, become 2nd Duke and Duchess
1740s	Bulstrode House is altered for William, 2nd Duke of Portland by Stiff Leadbeater
1750s	The Duchess becomes great friends with the celebrated artist and botanist Mrs Delaney
1761	2nd Duke dies. The Duchess creates a vast collection of botanical and geological specimens, especially shells - exotic animals roam the grounds at Bulstrode
1771	Captain Cook and Joseph Banks visit Bulstrode bringing seeds from their voyage
1770s	King George III, Queen Charlotte and The Prince of Wales visit Bulstrode from Windsor
1780s	After the Duchess' death, her collection of 4000 items is sold off, including the Portland Vase - William Henry Bendinck, the 3rd Duke, becomes Prime Minister twice

1750

1800

1806-9	Bulstrode House is remodelled by James Wyatt - the Pigeon Tower (Keep) dates from this period - Humphry Repton is the landscape architect - 3rd Duke dies 1809
1809	Bulstrode is sold to the 11th Duke of Somerset, Edward Adolphus Seymour
1831	The Duke was Bearer of the Orb at William IV's coronation and again at Victoria's (1838)
1841	The Duke rents Bulstrode to George Reid for £157 per year
1855	11th Duke dies. In 1856, Louisa and Anna-Maria Reid (George's sisters) request that the 12th Duke grant land for St James Church, which was inaugurated in 1859
1860's	The 12th Duke, also named Edward Adolphus Seymour, employs architect Benjamin Ferry to completely rebuild the house in gothic style - this is the present house
1871	The census records Bulstrode with 25 house servants, 20 gardeners, 9 grooms, 2 bricklayers, 2 sawyers and 2 carpenters, suggesting this was Bulstrode's heyday

1850

1900

1883	Duke dies - daughter Lady Helen Guendolen inherits with husband Sir John Ramsden
1906	Railway comes to Gerrards Cross - Bulstrode is a popular tourist attraction for Londoners
1913	In Congo CT Studd and Alfred Buxton begin the *Heart of Africa Mission* - later called WEC
1914	Sir John Frecheville Ramsden inherits Bulstrode - Bulstrode Park Hospital runs until 1915
1920s	Sir John Frecheville replants formal gardens with azaleas, rhododendrons, rare trees etc
1932	The estate and furniture are sold off to pay debts - house remains unsold
1939	WW2 - WAAF (Women's Auxiliary Air Force) School of Instruction held at Bulstrode
1941-5	Andover RAF Staff College at Bulstrode - Montgomery and Eisenhower visit Bulstrode
1958	The Bruderhof Community purchase Bulstrode and stay until 1966
1967	WEC International purchase Bulstrode and move HQ from Highland Road, London
	The events of this book take place in this period. If you have connections with WEC, add the date when your connection began *(e.g. Paul and Rose Harvey join WEC in 1992)*
	Your connection... →

1950

2000

2010	The International Leadership Team of WEC relocates from Bulstrode to Singapore
2016	WEC International (UK) relocate from Bulstrode to other parts of the country

Occupancy:

- Bulstrode Family
- Thomas Gomer
- Ambrose Bennett
- Judge Jeffreys
- Bendinck Family Dukes of Portland
- Seymour Family Dukes of Somerset
- Ramsden Family
- WAAF/RAF
- Bruderhof
- WEC International

Then and Now - the House on a Hill

"Bulstrode Park is remarkably extensive, yet it is still more remarkable for not containing a single level acre; being composed of perpetual swells and slopes, improved by scattered plantations, disposed with such admirable taste, as to form, on the whole, one of the most delightful parks in the kingdom." (18th Century quote)

above: copy of an engraving by Walker from an original by Corbould, 1794, donated to Bulstrode by Eddie and Phyllis Smith
below: Rose Harvey standing in a similar position to the picnic party above - January 2016

Bulstrode 1897

Atrium
1980s

Atrium
2015

PART ONE SEASONS

opposite page: *photos of Bulstrode Park and House in 1897 taken by Miss Rosamund Ramsden (when aged 26), daughter of Sir John William Ramsden and Lady Helen Guendolen Ramsden*

clockwise from top left: *Entrance Hall (Atrium), Pigeon Tower (Keep), Cedar of Lebanon,* Verandah, the Long Water, the Iron Gate into the garden (no longer exists)*

**this was the largest of the Cedars in Bulstrode Park; until recently it was standing in the grounds of WEC's neighbour, but sadly it fell in a storm during the winter of 2014/15*

Then and Now...
above: Dawn Redwood tree in the Bulstrode garden, taken in the 1970s and again from the same spot in 2015
below: the wheelbarrow and tool shed, early 80s and 2015

photo: WEC archives

photo: WEC archives

Then and Now

left: the entrance from the A40 taken in the 1980s (photo: Neil Rowe, WEC archives)

below: the A40 entrance, 2015

As many visitors using a GPS have discovered, this is the only vehicle entrance to Bulstrode. For some reason, SATNAVs still lead many a visitor on a wild goose chase via Hedgerley Lane to the Poynders Cottages entrance, even though it hasn't been used for Bulstrode since the days of horse and carriage!

left: the entrance gates at the top of the driveway, taken in the 1980s (photo: Neil Rowe, WEC archives)

below: same gates, 2015. Note how the speed limit has doubled in 30 years!

These gates are locked every night at 10:30pm by the person on "lock-up duty," and unlocked by the first person through the next morning.

It's mind-boggling to contemplate the numbers of mission-minded people that have passed through these gates during the last five decades.

Then and Now

right: the flats near the front gate when WEC came to view the property in 1966

below: the flats, home to various WEC families, in 2016

Including children there have been approximately 70 people in residence at Bulstrode in recent years, living in the flats, the new houses and in flats or rooms in the Main Building.

right: storage sheds out the back behind the Warehouse, demolished to make way for....

below: ...the new houses which were constructed in 2009 to accommodate families, couples and single workers

The style and material of the new houses - the colour of the bricks and mortar, the steep incline of the roof and the roof edgings - were chosen deliberately to match those of the main Bulstrode house.

The Changing Seasons

this page: the Lime Avenue, the Keep in spring, the Lily Pond in spring and winter
opposite page: Dawn Redwood (metasequioa glyptostroboides) in all four seasons

winter will always turn to spring and then to summer...

the Keep

the Beauty Walk

Palms and Swamp Cypress

Liquid Amber

"You will go out in joy and be led forth in peace; the mountains and hills will burst into song before you, and all the trees of the field will clap their hands."
Isaiah 55:12

Palm Trees

Japanese Acer

Tulip Tree

Silver Birches

Liquid Amber

Scots Pine

Coral Root

Forget-me-not

"See how the lilies of the field grow. They do not labour or spin. Yet I tell you that not even Solomon in all his splendour was dressed like one of these."

(Matthew 6:28-29)

Magnolia Fruit

Handkerchief Tree

Daffodils

Naked Ladies

Ginkgo Biloba or Maidenhair Tree

Magnolia

Rhododendron

"When morning dawns and evening fades You bring forth songs of joy." (Psalm 65:8)

the Bulstrode Lily Pond early morning (above) and in the evening (below)

above: the two banners hanging in the Bulstrode Chapel capture the essence of what Bulstrode is all about - they were made and donated to WEC by Tina Milne and her banner group in Harrogate (texts: Isaiah 56:7 and Psalm 96:3)

Prayer at the Core

Jeremy Ellis

WEC has always had prayer at its core, and prayer has always been part of life at Bulstrode.

I have heard many WEC retirees* fondly recall their days at Bulstrode and the times when everyone was called together to pray about an issue that needed to be worked through. Prayer was known to be the way forward. *(*retired WEC missionaries)*

I have learnt much about prayer from the retirees, particularly during their Annual Conference at Bulstrode. One retiree recalled a prayer meeting she'd been in where someone was praying, "Lord, brush away the cobwebs *(the hindrances)*" and someone else prayed out, "Kill the spider!" The importance of getting to the root cause!

When I came to Bulstrode for my interview to join WEC in 1989, I remember sitting after lunch with staff members who, as was their habit, opened Operation World *(see p. 36)* and prayed for the country of the day. Prayer has been woven through the lives and ministry of so many at Bulstrode, whether in groups or with prayer partners or in large meetings, and with changing patterns as the people living at Bulstrode have come and gone.

We'll never fully know the impact of praying people at Bulstrode on the progress of the gospel around the world. But this we do know... it has definitely made a difference.

"Solid, lasting missionary work is done on our knees."
James Fraser
(who worked among the Lisu people group in China)

Since moving with my family to Bulstrode in 2010, there have been a variety of prayer-related initiatives alongside the regular morning Chapel times...

*A new **Prayer Room** was set-up in a room above the front door with views of the grounds and the front driveway, and with a world map covering one complete wall. *(opposite below)*

*The **noticeboard** opposite the Dining Room was changed and used not for rotas and lists but instead as a changeable display to stimulate prayer for the nations.

*Evening **prayer meetings** were arranged and those in the local churches invited to join in praying for key issues around the world. More recently, a daily evening prayer time has been established, praying systematically through Operation World.

*A **Prayer Walk** leaflet was produced to help those wanting their walk in the grounds to be a more prayerful experience. Over all the years, many people have "done business" with God in the Bulstrode grounds - lives put right; decisions made; tears shed; callings confirmed; deep issues brought before the Throne of Grace.

*An **18-foot high cross** was erected in the grounds, cut from two fallen trees. It is visible from several angles, catching the attention of those wandering round the Beauty Walk. *(below)*

"Prayer is the life of missions. Continual and believing prayer is the secret of the life-giving power and fruitfulness of mission work. The God of missions is the God of prayer."
Andrew Murray

Since May Day 2008, Charles Cavenagh has regularly travelled from his home in Ealing to share in Bulstrode prayer meetings. He writes: I well remember the first Wednesday evening I came as Shely Ganguly read and performed the account of the raising of Lazarus in a most moving way. I continued attending when the meetings were changed to Tuesday mornings and I've always found the presentations most interesting and enlightening. It's been a privilege to pray with those who are involved full time in mission around the world. I have certainly benefited from this exposure and I'm grateful for the welcome I've always received.

The Gospel in a Garden

Dave Northcote

What part has a mansion like Bulstrode played in mission?

My first encounter was at a Mission and Me event held over a weekend in 1989 and I still remember the effect of seeing this place and thinking, "How on earth do these Christians have the faith to live in a place like this without salaries?"

In 2005 I returned from the Far East where I had served with WEC for 12 years with my two adult sons and my terminally ill wife. The first time Bulstrode had appeared as a place of wonder and challenge but this time it represented the place of peace and reassurance. Over the following weeks, whilst visiting my wife in hospital, I would return each day to the magnificent grounds where I was given responsibility to organise a team of Voluntary Helpers to keep the gardens in order.

Would God bring healing at this late hour to a condition that was beyond the ability of the doctors to cure? Such thoughts would tussle for my attention but then I'd be gripped by the vibrancy of all the many species of tree and shrub imported from so many countries around the world where the missionaries were taking the gospel. Then it struck me that God was speaking to me through His creation and as I paid attention to what he showed me, this is what I heard...

"You see that magnificent Turkey Oak, a good head and shoulders taller than the surrounding woodland? You thought you were like that tree once with all the advantages I gave you in your formative years - but where was I in your heart then?"

The following winter that tree came crashing down one still night after tiny flakes of snow had built up upon the branches and over it went revealing its rotten connection to the earth for the first time. "This is how your life might have been if you hadn't had a crisis and called out for Me to save you."

"Have you ever considered the scrawny Oak that no one looks at until the bluebell season?" As I began to take in its underwhelming presence it struck a chord with what the Lord had done with my life since I first came up the drive to Bulstrode. I noticed that it grew in a spot that was often waterlogged - and this was the reason it had become stunted, throwing its branches down to the ground, but whenever spring arrived it provided the ideal conditions for bluebells to thrive. I reflected on those years overseas where I had felt that conditions were not in my favour, floundering with a difficult language, never blending in to a culture that seemed to have turned all my expected norms on its head. Yet this was the very place the Lord blessed me and I saw new people enter God's Kingdom and thrive in a way that could not be explained by my own skill or gifting. It was as if those conditions that served as a disadvantage to me actually removed a barrier of acceptance to the gospel.

"Why do you suppose I confused the languages and scattered the peoples at Babel, whilst desiring to use those I would save to take the gospel to the nations? Did you not have to spend weeks and months listening and comprehending before you had the ability to speak? Did it not leave you in no doubt that it was My Spirit at work in you?"

"...the scrawny Oak...whenever spring arrived it provided the ideal conditions for bluebells to thrive..."

a duck's nest 30 ft above the ground in the bole of a Cedar tree that had been struck by lightning

photo: D Northcote

Cherry blossom

the fallen Oak trunk which provided a "place of comfort"

the magnificent Turkey Oak before it fell photo: D Northcote

"I know you are concerned about what will happen to the wife that I gave you; come and see the trunk of this Oak lying on its side and stripped of all signs of life. What do you think of that?" I have to say that at that point I only saw an object that needed clearing away. Taking my chainsaw to its branches it wasn't long before I needed to take a rest. It was while sitting on a sawn log that I began to contemplate the fact that although now dead, its usefulness had only just begun. The log had provided me with a place of comfort that would not have been the case while living.

"So you see...My death was intended to be your comfort in the face of death. I am the resurrection and the life. He who believes in Me will live, even though he dies; and whoever lives and believes in Me will never die. Do you believe this?" This came so personally to me at this point that I knew there were purposes in His mind that were greater than my wife's recovery.

The garden may have provided the backdrop for this encounter but the fellowship of fellow workers, the times of prayer and the focus on the wider work of WEC were all invaluable for maintaining perspective and for experiencing His love for me in a tangible way. Over the years since, I have conducted tours of the grounds and shared this story with many prospective workers and visitors alike.

Postscript

After my wife's home call I returned to the group of believers in the Far East where I had served. One of the older men told me after the meeting that they had been praying earnestly for her recovery and when that didn't happen he thought my life and faith would be in tatters. My joyful countenance had so impressed him that he could say that all I had sought to teach him regarding the resurrection must be true!

photo: courtesy Savills

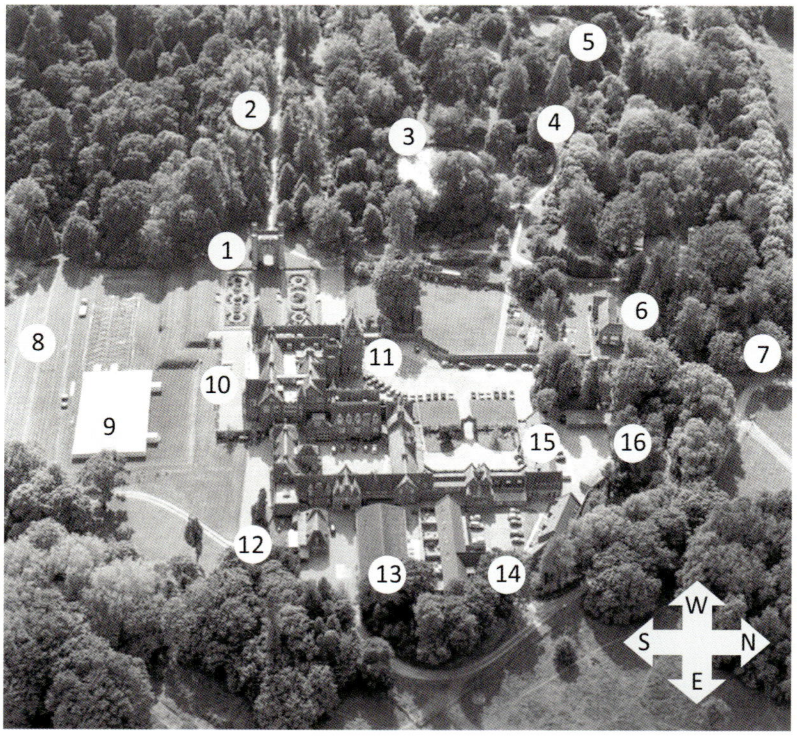

Bird's Eye View of Bulstrode

1 Keep
2 Lime Avenue
3 Lily Pond
4 Dawn Redwood
5 Beauty Walk
6 Flats near the Gate
7 Driveway to A40
8 South Lawn
9 The Marquee for GOFest meetings (temporary)
10 Verandah
11 Main Entrance
12 Nursery/Playground
13 Warehouse
14 New Houses
15 Stables Wing
16 Garages

PART TWO

60s and 70s

below: map showing the location of Bulstrode Park to the west of London

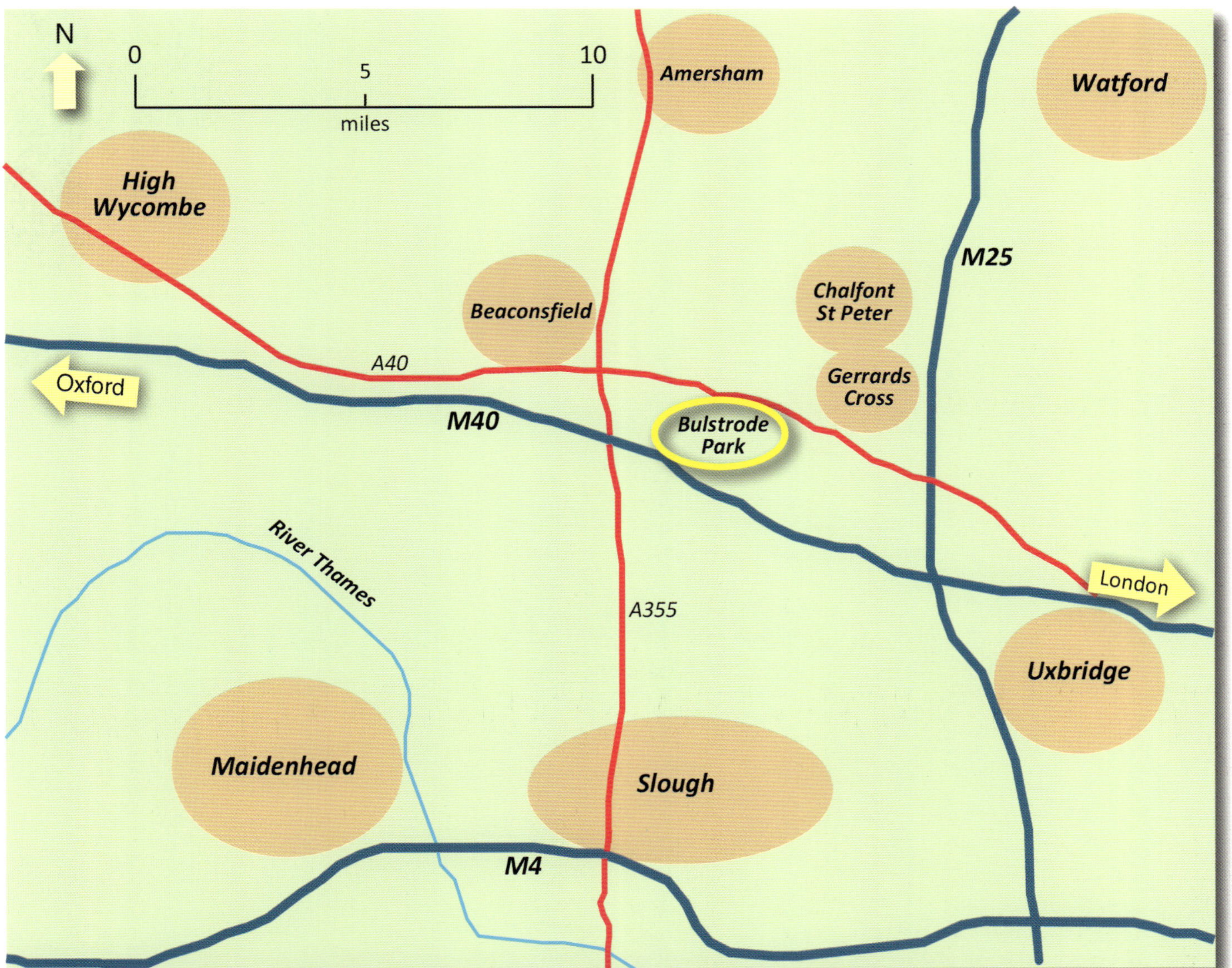

New Property

Arthur Ferdinando

Between September 1965 and June 1967 I was a student at the WEC Missionary Training College in Glasgow and it was during this period that the old WEC Headquarters in Upper Norwood was compulsory purchased and WEC had to find a new property.

From my recollections this took quite a time and I can remember it was a frequent subject for prayer among the students and staff at that time. On one occasion I remember Len Moules, the then British Director, coming up to Glasgow and taking a devotional meeting for the students and staff. He showed a letter which he had in the inside pocket of his jacket - everyone was far more formal in those days - which was from a WEC worker who was against the Mission going to Bulstrode. Len told us that he purposely had not opened the letter for he knew that it would disturb him before he spoke to us students. Presumably this WECer was in the minority as Bulstrode was duly purchased.

I left college and spent a year at another college in Watford, so as it was near Bulstrode I was able to visit those with whom I had spent time in Glasgow. They were now on their Candidate Orientation Course. I even learnt how to ride a motor bike on the Bulstrode driveway but that is another story.

I remember going to the yearly meetings which were held on Easter Monday in the Warehouse; the numbers of people attending then were obviously not as great as have come in more recent years to May Day and latterly to GOFest. They were good meetings and well worth attending. Edna and I lived near Dartford in Kent and John Leveson organised the trip. We (Edna, myself and our three sons) were the first ones to be picked up and the last to be dropped off on the return journey. I am glad to say that the boys went to Bulstrode when they were young and one of them is now serving God in Asia.

They were good days and the yearly trip to Bulstrode was something to be looked forward to; in many ways how I wish I could turn the clock back to such times!

right: various Easter Monday leaflets

below: the Worldwide Magazine, issue May/June 1967, announcing the purchase of Bulstrode

WORLD WIDE

GENESIS— *The home of Mr. and Mrs. C. T. STUDD, 17 Highland Road, London, S.E.19, was the first headquarters.*

THE PROMISED LAND— *The new W.E.C. Headquarters at "BULSTRODE", Gerrards Cross, Buckinghamshire. Fifty-four years of growth made visual. A house of 14 rooms and staff of 3 gives way to the new home of about 114 rooms, a staff for 8 departments, their children, candidates and missionaries.*

The old Keep and the Lime Avenue leading to the lake.

GENESIS–EXODUS

—AND THE PROMISED LAND

The searching, seeking and investigating of three and a half years is over.

The legal business settled, now we can reveal that the Compulsory Purchase Order which disturbed our peace is actually pressing the Crusade to new adventure as well as to a new building.

Another great moment in W.E.C. history has been reached. Advance adds a spring to the step and fresh horizons to vision.

The story and prospects are covered on pages 4 and 5.

No. 306 6d. MAY—JUNE, 1967

WORLDWIDE EVANGELIZATION CRUSADE

Dedication

John Leveson

Bulstrode Dedication: It was my privilege and pleasure to be at the Dedication Service of Bulstrode in 1967. The week in which it took place Jack and Rose Robertson - on furlough from Upper Volta (now Burkina Faso) - were staying with us, and the three of us travelled on a Timpson's coach organised by Lionel Hemmings of Bromley. Lionel was the architect who advised WEC on the purchase of the property. The actual dedication service was held at the bottom of the staircase in the Entrance Hall. Some work had been done on the pillars but there was obviously still a lot to be done at that time.

In the late 1960s, there was not the car ownership that there is today and from that angle Bulstrode was somewhat cut off and rather like a monastery. To help people, especially families, Jean Walker who was on the staff at that time, ran a shop in one of the rooms in the East Wing Corridor. If I remember correctly it operated for a good few years, and we enjoyed having a browse around it on our visits to Bulstrode.

Tragedy: A couple or so years later In 1969, Bessie Brierley and Quirino Baro were tragically killed in a road accident in Scotland. I can remember the funeral service being held at Gold Hill Church with the internment taking place at Parkside Cemetery. This entailed us all crossing the busy A40. There were so many vehicles following the hearse, including a coach, that the police stopped the traffic on the A40 to let everybody get through.

Open Days: These started off as Easter Monday meetings before they were moved to the May Day Bank Holiday. In their heyday it was great seeing between 15 and 20 coaches, plus minibuses in front of the house, as well as all the cars in the field just outside the main gates. For some reason (maybe desperation!), I had the privilege of being head steward in the marquee for several years. The year Brother Yun was the main speaker was, I think, the worst one for weather, yet people were queuing up in the pouring rain as the marquee was full, so that they could get in for the next meeting. At the bottom of the drive, the police were turning cars away because there was no more room. *(see p. 66)*

A little incident: One Saturday we had been invited to visit the then British Director and his wife. Their son was going out with the daughter of the treasurer from another Mission whom he had met at university and who came from our area. He was busy making some jam. Half way through he took a phone call from his girlfriend and he forgot completely about the jam on the stove!

scenes from the Dedication Day (above) and Open Days

photos: WEC archives

This Could Be a Great Scheme

A letter from Norman Singleton to Len Moules (then WEC Director) written in 1966 outlining the potential of Bulstrode.

238 Turney Road,
Dulwich Village,
London S.E.21.

Saturday, 17th September, 1966.

Dear Len,

BULSTRODE PARK

It occurs to me that it may assist your colleagues on Tuesday if you have the enclosed particulars and plans. Also, I perhaps should briefly set down my present feelings on the subject. I am having to do this at home - hence the plain paper.

Structure. A partial survey should be made, particularly as to roofs, electrical work, rot and woodworm. The main building is 100 years old, and appears to have stood well.

Maintenance. This must be substantial; but you are getting substantial accommodation.

Running Costs These should be reasonable, except perhaps in regard to heating. Again, you cannot have so much accommodation without much running costs

Services There is plenty of electricity, but NO GAS. Gas cannot be brought without very great initial expense The drainage is by cesspool only, but appears to work. Water is pumped from a well, except for the new flats. (The particulars are misleading)

Planning position This land is in the Green Belt and the subject of a binding Agreement between the Society and the Planning Authority. I expect no difficulty in obtaining consent for your use, even if such consent is necessary at all. You would be permanently restricted from major alterations in use and character.

Suitability Location is excellent, except that you would need a mini-bus. I think you could make a pleasing H.Q. and home here and that the disadvantages are out weighed by the great advantages. Some of the divided rooms should be restored to original form.

Summarising I cannot quarrel with the asking price of £75,000. The main building wants generally making more attractive internally. Smaller parts might be better demolished, with T.P. consent.

The industrial parts will be a waste of money unless you use them. The total upkeep will be too much unless you fill the premises with people and work. Accordingly, I consider the matter turns upon your being able to make good use of practically the whole place by bringing printing and other work under the one roof. This could be a great scheme.

Yours sincerely,

(signed) Norman (Singleton)

cartoon of "Moving Day" from Highland Road to Bulstrode

photos of the first visit to Bulstrode

below: the first large conference to be held at Bulstrode - International Leaders' Conference 1969 - a few of the participants are named - some of you reading this will remember more of these faithful servant leaders of WEC

What is this Place?

Jean Goodenough

Jean's tract, illustrated by Connie Lyne photos: J Goodenough

I have many memories of Bulstrode, both from my Candidate days in 1974 and from working there for a number of years after my return from Africa (1986 onwards).

Maria Baro was the receptionist while I was a Candidate. At that time Reception was situated in what later became the Coffee Lounge *(and then the Terrace Room - see photo opposite)*. This gave a great view of the front door, but not much else. I think Maria must have been about to go on holiday and for some reason I was selected to learn her job. Answering the phone involved flicking switches up and down to make connections and was quite complicated. However, I survived.

Years later, when I returned to Bulstrode I was given a choice of jobs and opted for Reception simply because I had done it before, though the telephone system no longer involved flicking switches. By this time, Reception had moved to the Book Room area. I had to endure all the noise of the old Reception desk being dismantled; not easy when you're trying to answer the phone.

Many strangers came into the building, approached Reception, and asked exactly the same question: "What is this place, anyway?" It happened so often that I wrote a cartoon-style tract, illustrated by Connie Lyne, which answered that question.

On one occasion the visitor turned out to be a Jehovah's Witness. On discovering that Bulstrode was the Headquarters of a Missionary Society she demanded that I call everyone in the building together so that she could address them! I refused, but did call someone to come and talk to her.

Another visitor expressed great interest in the building, especially its maintenance. It turned out he was a man

specialising in woodwork who hoped that Bulstrode might have some jobs that he could do. I explained that most of the work was done by volunteers, at which point he asked the usual questions. He wanted to leave a flyer in case we might need his services in the future but suddenly became very embarrassed, saying he hadn't had our kind of organisation in mind when he had thought up his eye-catching title for the flyer: "Adult male stripper reveals all!"

A different kind of incident that stands out in my memory happened on a Sunday when I was on weekend duty. As usual, Reception was unmanned on a Sunday morning, so no one saw who entered the building, leaving a small package on the desk. It was around the time when parcel bombs were being sent and it was disconcerting that the only marks on it were the letters IRA and IRAA! When I saw it, I lifted it carefully, listened for ticking and shook it gently. Nothing. But I still didn't trust it. Later, Pauline Nicholas came to relieve me on Reception and I asked her what she thought of the package, but didn't voice my fears about it. She reckoned we should open it. I took off the paper to reveal a small wooden box. Cautiously, I lifted the lid and was relieved to see a handwritten note to say that the contents were a gift to WEC to use as we wished. Underneath were tight rolls of pink notes. I thought it was foreign currency, and was stunned to discover that they were British £50 notes, a denomination that I had never seen before.

Pauline called her husband, asking him to come to Reception at once without telling him what the matter was. I can still picture Colin walking up to us with a concerned expression on his face. He took the box to the Finance Office and called Jenny Carter to help him count the money. She retells the story in *Beyond the Edge (Evan Davies, page 116)*. Between them, Colin and Jenny counted £26,000 that day (a *huge* sum in the late 1980s)!

above: the Main Entrance Hall (now Atrium) c.1968

Bulstrode Visit

John Gravett

Sheila and I were married in July 1967 and at the time we were both full-time workers with Christian Literature Crusade. The management of the London shop, which was then in Ludgate Hill, was my responsibility and Sheila was one of the book shop staff. We lived at 3 Highland Road, Upper Norwood which was a WEC property just down the road from the WEC Headquarters, 19 Highland Road. This was a well appointed building having a hall for meetings and other rooms for offices and accommodation. Other WEC properties were situated in the neighbourhood. *Radio Worldwide* was in Harold Road and we remember visiting the sound studios there which at the time were sound-proofed with egg boxes even though the equipment was state of the art.

Facilities for WEC were scattered and smaller than the developing and expanding Mission required. Bulstrode was acquired and several of us went on a visit one evening to see this exciting and challenging acquisition for the future UK Headquarters of WEC. Approaching Bulstrode via the drive, the rural and expansive nature of the Bulstrode estate was impressive and drawing close to the buildings only added to the wonder of the site. The place was spectacular and magnificent compared to 19 Highland Road which could have fitted easily into one of the quadrangles of Bulstrode with room to spare.

Excitement and wonder mounted as we came in through the Main Entrance and into the hall and stairwell. The place seemed huge but as the run-down condition of the place sank into awareness, we realised what an incredible challenge this was going to be; the work that would need to be done; the finances required to see it through; and the time and effort it would take. The task promised to be impossible.

Personally, I wondered what they had taken on. BUT - WEC had embarked on this journey in faith and this was simply another challenge to be overcome. Seeing what has been accomplished over the last fifty years in making the place a centre of excellence and turning it into a vibrant mission headquarters and sending base has really been awe inspiring. God is amazing and when people rise to such a challenge it only honours and exalts Him all the more.

The First Bulstrode Candidate Course

Flora Gibson and Moira Leslie

In January 1968 the first group of Candidates started their six month Candidate Course *(CC)* at Bulstrode. The four Swiss Candidates completed their course in Switzerland. There were five others too. Four had gone through Missionary Training College *(MTC)* in Glasgow together. The Swiss ladies shared a room with an English teacher who was there to teach them English, but they ended up teaching her Swiss German instead!

The decor of Bulstrode when purchased was dark and dingy. Part of the course work was to see the rooms transformed to being bright and cheerful. We had shared rooms and the privilege of going down to the Basement and choosing the colours to paint our own rooms. The importance placed on attending morning Chapel and "Prayer Battery"* meant that we had a sense of oneness with those on the fields. It was a time when we knew all the WEC missionaries and where they worked. We learnt, as Candidates, that "prayer requests" were taken really seriously by the WEC HQ. *(*as the prayer meetings were then called)*

It was a privilege to be alongside missionaries who had worked in Congo like Eric and Daisy Smith, who were our Candidate Secretaries, and Leslie and Bessie Brierley who had worked in Portuguese Guinea. Bessie and Daisy were often in the Bulstrode Kitchen preparing meals, helped by the lady Candidates. The lady Candidates needed to pay attention to how much went into the soup depending on who was cooking. Bessie was extravagant and Daisy was frugal!

Jean Walker *(photo p. 89)*, an Irish/Canadian home from Liberia, was the driver at the time. Jean took people to and from the airports. Jean teased people. She was larger than life with a great sense of humour, and she also had a shop packed with sweets, coffee/tea, biscuits, writing paper and pens etc, plus radios and tape recorders and bargains that she had picked up from "Cash & Carry" for the Bulstrode Fellowship. Jenet Jones, a Welsh lady in her 60s was the Accommodation Secretary. Jenet* usually wore a blue overall and would be heard singing as she walked up and down the corridors. There were not so many guest rooms in those days, but Jenet would always say that she had a spare bed up her sleeve! *(*Jenet is the Welsh spelling of Janet)*

the impressive Entrance Hall (later Atrium)

It was such a privilege to meet special visitors and people passing through to countries like Libya and Ivory Coast. Corrie Ten Boom came and spoke to the Candidates. None of the Candidates had a car, so we either walked across the fields to Gold Hill Baptist Church or went by minibus each Sunday. David Pawson was the minister there at that time.

the back of the Bulstrode Kitchen - note the ladder up to the "Minstrels' Gallery"

Bulstrode Memories

Meg Northcote

Many memories come flooding back since the first time I visited Bulstrode in 1969 as a CLC *(Christian Literature Crusade)* Candidate. It was then a place in much need of renovation but the atmosphere was impressive to one entering into mission. Talking and hearing stories of folks who had been overseas for many years and now ready to serve and trust the Lord in this new situation, I saw courage and faith that spurred me on in those early days.

Over the years there have been many visits, having transferred to WEC in 1988. The majority of those years I worked alone and to come to Bulstrode was always a joy as it was like "home" with the warm welcome from many folks. Having just visited teams in the ME and NA *(Middle East and North Africa)* it was good to share the burdens with those who had been praying whilst I was on those trips; these were precious times of fellowship. I always came away encouraged and uplifted that I had such a wonderful family supporting me. Hearing each other's testimonies of His grace and provision strengthened one's faith for the challenges ahead.

The willingness of folks to take me to Heathrow Airport at unsociable hours always impressed me, as so often I left for those overseas visits from Bulstrode. Arriving once very late at night from Heathrow, the person who had met me there invited me back to their flat for supper so that they could hear about the trip and teams I had visited. This left a deep impression in my mind of their commitment to the Lord.

The place is impressive on arrival, but for me it's been some of the amazing people I have met inside that have made the deepest impression and challenged my faith and walk with the Lord.

The Big Move

Jo Parnell

A black bin liner and a spade... this is one of my memories from being on the Candidates' Course in 1967. Pauline (Nicholas), myself and perhaps others were taken from the old WEC HQ in Highland Road for a few days at a time to help prepare Bulstrode for the "Big Move." We never really had a proper Candidate Course but it was good training for life on the mission field. What a change from cleaning the old HQ Hostel which was always clean, to shovelling into bin liners the ceilings which had been torn down in the East Wing because of deathwatch beetle. In the Main Courtyard was a pile of old oil heaters which had been used by the former occupants to heat that enormous building.

"The Move" was prepared with military precision by our UK Director, ex-Army Major Len Moules. Nearly every article of furniture was labelled with a Bulstrode room or the Warehouse number. Pickford's Vans moved us. They had to be of the right size to pass through the main gates. Years later when my mother moved home, one of the Pickford's removal men remembered moving WEC to Bulstrode!

There were lovely walks in the grounds and we could go anywhere and pick anything. A tree house, a Teddy Bear House and a swing from the branch of a tree which swung over the big lake were fun. Bulstrode grounds in the snow were a truly wonderful sight.

"...a truly wonderful sight..."

Place of Blessing

Glen Osborne

I was thinking of the first time I ever visited Bulstrode. Neil Rowe took me and a Candidate from New Zealand out from Highland Road to visit the property. You will have seen the photos of what it looked like then before all the building and renovations. I remember thinking...a lot of people have a lot more faith than I have!

Then over the years what a blessing that place has been to us. On our first furlough when we came home battered and bruised we arrived for the Annual Staff Conference. A communion service in the Dining Room was packed and the singing and being there just left us crying the whole time. We had not had this at this stage in Senegal. God ministered through people and in that place.

All through the years as we travelled via Bulstrode either going or coming, there was special personal blessing to us and rich fellowship with all the family there. Bulstrode has been a place of renewal and blessing for us as it has for so many others too.

Lost and Found

Liz Cleak

My first memory of Bulstrode is of being lost! Would I ever find my room and bed? In 1971 we were staying there for a youth camp reunion, and late in the evening I went visiting to the room of a Candidate. We'd met when I attended evening courses at Birmingham Bible Institute. It was a lovely chat but I had no idea how to return to my own room. Happily, in my bewilderment I was found and led safely roomwards by a Bulstrode resident. But that evening chat sealed a relationship that lasted through the years when she supported and prayed for me when I went overseas, although ill health meant that she never made it to Nepal.

By 1974 I was a Candidate for WEC myself, no longer lost in the corridors as I'd cleaned most of the guest rooms. It was a delight to work in the Laundry alongside Jenet Jones, a Welsh lady who sang as she worked and blessed me with her positive attitude and encouragements. *(Jenet is on the left in the picture below)*

We needed to up stakes and move to another room, they told us. Why? The plumbers were coming ... at least, that's what we understood. Well, our room was above the warm Laundry drying rooms so we weren't too thrilled, but no doubt they would work on the boilers. We laughed when we discovered that the "plumbers" were in fact the Plummer family, arriving to take over as Managers.

As we drew closer to the time of leaving England, Linda Townsend (now Chamberlain) and I were thinking of some things we would miss when living in the tropics. We hatched a plan to get up very early and record the dawn chorus, taking our little cassette tape recorder out among the trees of the grounds. The birds sang beautifully for us, but when we came to listen to the tape we discovered that we also had a constant hum of background noise from the M40 - yes, even then! It was a lesson to me of how we can become so accustomed to some things that we tune them out, unless God points them out to us. The tape is lost long years past, but the lesson remains.

mops at the ready   photo: WEC archives

The Bulstrode Chimneys

Wilf Urquhart

When we did our Candidates' Course *(CC)* in 1971, permission had just been granted by the local council to remove the 6-foot tall chimneys that were on the top of all the chimney breasts. These chimneys were in blocks of four, five or six sitting on a stone breast. Permission was granted because they were in very poor condition and posed a significant danger. If one had fallen it would have gone right through the roof and caused no end of damage. Each chimney would have weighed around half a ton and they were made with red bricks. After each chimney had been removed, a large slate was placed over the hole and weighed down with a brick.

This was quite an undertaking as no hydraulic equipment was available for the job. Dick Tumber was in charge of the practical teams and he organised us into teams. Scaffolding had to be erected around each chimney in order to begin the task of removing the brickwork. As none of us had experience working with scaffolding we proceeded with much prayer and discussion. Those who had a head for heights were elected to work at the top and others at various different levels depending on their degree of vertigo. Some of the chimneys were in very dangerous condition and several were leaning alarmingly to the side. A large metal tube was erected as near as possible to the base of the chimney. This tube continued right down to ground level where it ended in a trailer. Once a brick began its journey down the tube it did so with alarming noise and ended up in the trailer with a loud bang and a cloud of dust. Some unfortunately, due to their great speed, bounced out of the trailer and landed quite some distance away. Wherever the trailer was parked, all cars had to be moved to a safe distance or run the risk of being bombed by flying bricks! We were by far the noisiest practical team during that CC.

Despite the danger attached to the job there were no significant accidents during the procedure. Just one person ended up in hospital when he missed the brick with his hammer and hit his finger instead. Sadly he lost the new hammer he was using; it fell down the chimney and was never recovered. Every time we visit Bulstrode my eyes automatically go to the chimneys and I am reminded again of our CC.

now you see them...

above: the southwest facade, showing the chimneys before they were removed

below: the north facade, with chimneys still in place

...now you don't!

above: after Wilf and the gang had been at work

below: the north facade, no chimneys

left: close-up of chimneys

The Fat of the Land

Margaret White

I arrived in Bulstrode for CC *(Candidate Course)* around the end of September 1968. There wasn't nearly enough for the monthly allowances due to be sent to the mission fields. That first weekend, I saw WEC fellowship in action as together with the Bulstrode Staff we knelt before the Lord in the Staff Lounge about this matter. God was faithful, as always, and the money came in, I don't remember how.

Meantime, Bulstrode seemed so GRAND. It was not long after WEC had moved from Highland Road. Bulstrode was still a work in progress, but it was being done "to a high spec" in our eyes. And the meals? Amazing! Marvellous! None of us Candidates had come from "posh" backgrounds, yet here we were, eating meals with spuds, meat and SEVERAL VEG! Every day! We Candidates had a meeting about it. No money for the fields, and we were living on the fat of the land! Where was this life of sacrifice and fellowship we had heard about? We felt outrage.

Where was this life of sacrifice and fellowship we had heard about?!

Our hot-head spokesman told Eric and Daisy Smith (our Candidate Secretaries) what we thought...Nothing was said, but dear Mary Rowe quietly allocated the spokesman's wife and me to Kitchen Duty the very next day. That was when we saw our God SUPERABUNDANTLY, RICHLY SUPPLY CABBAGES AND CAULIFLOWERS AND MARROWS AND CARROTS AND VEG of every description by the van-load...as all the local churches in the posh Gerrards Cross area sent the produce of their Harvest Thanksgiving to the only folk they could think of who might need it...us! No big freezers back then, so we cooked it as it came in. I can think of other things, but I'll leave others to tell of deathwatch beetle in the East Wing Corridor, or Jean Walker's shop...and other things.

below: Jean Walker's shop (photos c. 1968)

top right: the Lime Walk scene of Mavis's snake incident

Snake!

Mavis Rodger

I was soon to be Liberia-bound - my very first visit to Africa! In the Bulstrode Dining Room I was sitting with Helen from Holland. "Well," says I, "If I see a snake, I'll be on the first plane home!"

I left Helen to meet friend Debbie to go blackberry picking. I walked down the Lime Avenue and there wiggling across my path, as if on cue, was a little snake! I think the Lord arranged that! For wasn't I as likely to meet a snake in the Bulstrode grounds as in Liberia? I didn't freak out anyway!

So off I flew with the very first copies of the Mano New Testament in my luggage. I never did cut short my time in Liberia.

Horns of a Dilemma

Judy Brittenden

It was New Zealand, 1971, and Gerry had almost finished the major pack required for a family of five to travel from NZ to the UK and beyond. There was a loud knock at the Curate's house door. "Am I in time?" asked an excited member of our youth group. "This is my very first one and I want you to have it because it's special and it will bring you lots of blessing!" For once Gerry was lost for words.

And so it was that somehow a large set of antlers was stuffed into the very top of our last trunk. This was not because we had the remotest need for it in "darkest Africa" but because time was running out and we didn't know what else to do with it.

You know what it is like unpacking and sorting things in the depths of the Bulstrode Basement/dungeon. It is a case of groping around in the absence of light and air and getting the job done as quickly as possible. Well, on one of these occasions we must have been in a particular hurry...either that or especially careless. One item failed to make it back into our cases...

Imagine our surprise when on a return visit to Bulstrode some time later, we saw "our" antlers, mounted and resplendent, in the Reception porch. Gerry was thrilled. "How fitting!" he thought. He and John Adcock, having drawn the short straw, had years earlier been obliged to spend many uncomfortable hours sanding that jolly porch! Somehow it seemed only right that a Kiwi stag should be given a place of honour there...even if only for a passing moment.

Accepted into the Family

Jackie Rowe

I was a Candidate from September to December 1973; was given the right hand of fellowship by Robert Mackey when I was accepted into WEC in January 1974; and then, as we did in those days, stayed on at Bulstrode as an "accepted Candidate" for two more months. There were 17 on my Candidate Course - 3 Dutch, 1 South African and the rest British/Irish.

Bulstrode was a very close-knit community in those days and one of the best times of the week was a sing-song (hymns and choruses to guitar accompaniment) in the sitting area at the foot of the Main Stairs (now called the Atrium) after church on a Sunday evening. Staff, Candidates and visitors all joined in. Very few people had TVs in those days so I can remember lots of us crowding into Jenet Jones's room on 14th November 1973 to watch Princess Anne's wedding.

We ladies were definitely not allowed to wear trousers, except when the potatoes were ready for harvesting, when we were allowed to wear them as we scrabbled around in the dirt on our knees. Norman Grubb came on a visit and as well as speaking in Chapel to everyone, he spoke to the Candidates alone and encouraged us to be "free in Christ" and wear trousers whenever we wanted to. Since we all wanted to be accepted into WEC, we still didn't dare to!

I remember, too, all the hours of practical work, cleaning long corridors with buffing machines in the days before they were carpeted. So many happy memories; going out to the very extensive grounds for my morning quiet times, amazing talks in Chapel like Charlton Smith speaking about the "cups" in the Bible (e.g. cup of suffering, cup of blessing) illustrated by his own fabulous paintings, and then the many happy hours spent working the switchboard at weekends.

Of course, there were some hard times - the discipline was not always easy - but my overriding memories are of a sense of deep joy and even "awe" at being accepted as part of the WEC family.

A Wave and a Prayer

Judy Brittenden

It was the tradition in the early days, when missionaries were leaving for their field of service, for the "family" to gather on the front steps of Bulstrode to send them off with a kind of ceremonial "farewell wave." That moment for us remains clear in my mind.

Charlton (Smith), who had helped Gerry with the final pack of the overladen trailer the night before, had come early to bless our tiny VW Beetle with a final silent prayer. He was unusually quiet. The time had come. We drove slowly down the drive. I will always remember that as the group broke up to go about the business of the day one small figure remained resolute...his large white handkerchief fluttering like a dove's wings in the morning light, until we could see him no more.

Twenty-four hours later we were ascending a slope in the South of France when we noticed that the driver coming towards us had fallen asleep at his wheel. The collision was unavoidable. The front axle of our car was broken and one of our children was confined to hospital for five days.

The story of the way that God covered our needs during those days is too long to write here. However, there is one thing that needs to be said. Some weeks later we learned from dear Florence, that in the early hours of that fateful day and about five hours before our accident at 8am, Charlton was woken by the Lord who asked him to pray for our family. He had remained on his knees by his bed until the break of that day.

"What love..."

Jackie's Candidate Group:

left to right back row:

George Walker
Donald Graham
Mark Timmins
Tony Goodman
(Sue was absent)
Ron Harper

middle row:

Wendy Baldwin
Mary (later married Alan Rapley)
Angela (married Mark Timmins)
Marjorie Walker
Nella Heyboer
Jackie Tatum (later married Neil Rowe)
Margot ven Zuiden
Belle Purdy

front row:

Ria Korn
Hester Saunders
Amy Martin (later married Norman Cuthbert)

photo: courtesy J Rowe

Prayer, Work, Beauty

Evan and Jenny Davies

Evan and Jenny were WEC's Deputy International Directors from 1993-98 and International Directors from 1999-2004.

Story 1 - Answer to prayer!
As International Directors resident at Bulstrode we needed £400 to pay for our next plane trip to visit one of the WEC branches. We had been praying and trusting for some time. Nobody knew of our need. And now it was the day. In tears that morning we poured out heavy hearts to the Lord.

Evan went downstairs to start work in the Courtyard Office. On the way the leader of Unimatco *(see p. 53)*, John Chudley, met him and said: "By the way, Evan, I've just put £400 in your account at the WEC Finance Office. It's part of our tithe from the Unimatco ministry." What rejoicing we had that day and we can still remember with much thankfulness that amazing miracle which only the Lord could do.

Story 2 - Prayer, work and beauty.
Bulstrode was a ***prayer place***. We loved the weekly missionary prayer times and the special sessions at Annual Conferences. Jesus was there and we sensed Him at work. What a privilege to have a stream of missionaries from all over the world visiting on a daily basis sharing up-to-date prayer information. In our office we prayed each day - the work was too big to handle without God's help.

Bulstrode was a ***work place***. It was a case of "all hands on deck." From most recent Candidate or visitor to International Leader, all were rostered on daily duties - dishes, telephone answering, driving to Heathrow, turn in the Kitchen – these helped in teaching humility and enabled the family to get to know each other. Then there were the big projects that gave great opportunities to trust God and see Him at work. It was all about doing something for Jesus, taking fresh steps in knowing Him.

Bulstrode was a ***beautiful** place* with space to walk, share, think and pray. Every day and each season was different. It was a glorious setting for large events. Missionaries on furlough could have some precious moments to relax and recover. We loved having daily prayer walks round the Beauty Walk. God taught us so much at those times. He gave us peace in our hearts, eyes to see heavenly solutions to IO *(International Office)* issues, and challenged us to listen to His voice. The very location made it easier to think, learn, study and take advantage of the resources of the UK WEC and Operation World teams.

Story 3 - International episode.
WEC has changed and no more is it the European Mission Agency from the pith-helmet-brigade but a worldwide team from over 50 countries. Often there were new nationalities to meet at Bulstrode.

One day we had a visit of the Korean Board who were taken on a tour of the place and then shared in an introduction to what happens at Bulstrode. Board members were added to the daily duty lists. When asked to share their impressions, what had most challenged them was that UK Leaders, International Directors, Deputy Leaders and Bulstrode Managers were all doing duties. Also administrative and practical staff told how God had given them spiritual gifts in all the necessary areas of service. Wives of Board members were amazed to see the way the structure worked. God had given His servants praising hearts and a willingness to serve Him.

Azaleas by the Top Pond

God's Place for God's Time for God's Glory

Pauline Nicholas

When I think back over the years of my times in Bulstrode, the overwhelming sensation is thankfulness for God's faithfulness; His unfailing love and grace and His strength made perfect in our weakness. The task was big, too big for us, BUT GOD...

Part 1

I was a Candidate in 1967 and went to Bulstrode with other Candidates as part of the cleaning team. We stayed in the flats near the gate for a few days and cleaned the Laundry. Along with us was a team of men; missionaries on furlough and folk delayed from the field, all working and painting after the central heating had been put in and laying the floorboards before the floor covering was put down throughout the building. Everything had to be done. All the walls in the flats and large rooms had been painted in bright reds, orange, green and blue by the former owners. After the move we lady Candidates were allocated the Tower Room and in our time off between lectures, projects and practical work, we had to decorate our own rooms. All the staff did the same. The fellowship was very special.

We worked in the Kitchen with Bessie Brierley and Daisy Smith in turn directing us. During the first Staff Meeting at Bulstrode in the Upstairs Lounge we were "accepted" into WEC. We served at the first wedding...Carol Moules, a very special occasion. We saw staff work together and pray together for individuals, fields and situations; whatever the difficulty, staff met in the Lounge to pray. I returned in the summer to help and again after language study before going to Congo in November 1969.

Whatever the difficulty, staff met in the Lounge to pray...

Part 2

Colin and I married in Congo and went to Bulstrode on home leave for short visits. We felt very much part of the bigger family as they supported us in prayer and fellowship.

In 1975 we were invalided home with two small children and I was admitted to Mildmay Mission Hospital for many months. The fellowship cared for Colin and Sandra (aged 3) and Robert (18 months), surrounding them with love, prayer and support. Colin worked on the practical work, building walls before being asked to work in the Finance Office. What was meant to be a few months became five years. I, with lots of help from Voluntary Helpers, Candidates and staff, cared for the family and Colin became Finance Secretary. During this time Neil Rowe returned from a visit to Congo deeply challenged, having met God in a new way. There began a new spirit of seeking God and prayer as a result; a deepening sense of our need of Him and a longing to see God work in new ways in our lives and right through the Mission.

During these years everyone sought to reach out to our neighbours and those we worked with in the area. There were outreach open evenings with a gospel presentation at Christmas time *(right)* and the grounds were open for people to visit in the summer. There were special times at Christmas when those who were there got together on Christmas Eve and Christmas Day. The young people performed pantomimes and volunteers cooked the Christmas dinner for everyone. Numbers were quite small so everyone had to be involved in everything.

Part 3

After home leave in 1984, when we were based in Wales, we met with Neil and Mary Rowe. We were unable to return to Congo on medical grounds. Neil and Mary were also told on medical grounds to step down from leadership. I went into hospital for surgery and Colin went to Staff Conference where we were asked to pray about leadership of WEC UK. I struggled with staying in Britain and going to Bulstrode, but God met me in a special way in my hospital room. Was I willing to do His will and leave everything in His hands? As soon as I said "yes" to Him I had complete peace about the future. We moved to Bulstrode in August 1985 and settled in the flats and were there until 1996.

God answered so many prayers for the WEC family. At that time there were nine MK teenagers from all over Britain and the world; Jill Johnstone took them under her wing and helped them integrate together and into the community and church. We had a very steep learning curve. The team in the British Office were very important as we dealt with imprisonment of a worker; coups, accidents and many serious situations involving people and families; learning to trust God for His wisdom and grace in all the different situations; people and their many and varied needs passing through; and constantly changing situations.

The things that stand out are:

*meetings in the Reception area to farewell individuals and families going out all over the world, praying for them and sending them off in the minibus
*others returning with all the variety of needs
*prayer times, extended sessions, staff meetings, financial challenges
*God's amazing grace and love in all the different situations
*special occasions, such as the first parents' day, seeing the parents share with each other
*sharing the joy of weddings - and the celebrations of those who have gone on to Glory
*special occasions, such as visits from Corrie Ten Boom, George Verwer and many others
*special May Days with all the joys of meeting people - friends, new and old
*the love of the fellowship as we moved on and passed on the baton to Stewart and Jean Moulds in 1996

Bulstrode has been God's place for God's time for God's glory. God will complete what He has in mind so that the whole world will hear the good news of Jesus His Son.

To Him be all the glory!

photo: WEC archives

The Missionary Orientation Centre (MOC)

David and Anne Burnett

The 1970s was a decade that caused a radical rethink within mission organizations in the understanding of mission and its practice. This was especially seen at The **First International Congress on World Evangelization** held in Lausanne from 16th to 25th July, 1974. A key feature of the conference was a change in focus from looking at mission in terms of countries to that of "people groups." These developments resulted in considerable excitement in mission, but it became clear that in the UK there was a lack of training at Bible Colleges in this new understanding of mission strategy. It was for this reason that the Missionary Orientation Centre *(MOC)* was established at Bulstrode in July 1977.

The MOC programme, designed by David and Anne Burnett, consisted of a number of short courses of two or five weeks for those who had already studied the Bible and Theology. There were five courses of 5-weeks which together became the basis of the MOC year programme.

*First, ***Cultural Anthropology***, which provided tools in how to understand the way of life of a society and how to work in different cultures.

*Secondly, ***Church Growth*** took the principle of people groups to explore strategies that were relevant to the felt needs of a society and focussed upon church planting.

*A third course was a study of ***Muslim Societies***, which went beyond Islamic theology to look at how this impacted the way of life of Muslims and the various mission strategies that have been developed.

*Fourth, was a course on ***Mission and Development*** that explored the holistic approach to mission in both the rural and urban context.

photos: courtesy David Burnett

*Fifth, the study of ***Folk Religion*** held by animistic societies including those holding to such beliefs and practices but calling themselves Muslims, Buddhists, Hindus or even Christians.

The very first 5-week course had only 4 students and the class met in a small room in the Main House of Bulstrode. Later, as the student numbers increased, the programme was located in the stables area of Bulstrode which was redeveloped with library, offices and classroom facilities.

The first four students *(below)* illustrated some of the emerging trends in the 1980s. Only one of the four students was from WEC, while the others came from different organizations showing a trend towards **inter-Mission cooperation**. One student coming from Hong Kong and one from Korea typified the increasing **international nature** of mission. The Korean student had taken Biblical and Theological studies for five years in Korea prior to becoming a full-time pastor. To fulfil his call to cross-cultural mission he found the MOC ideally suited to his needs. During the following years a steady stream of Korean missionaries came to study at the MOC. A third trend was the **growth of short-term mission**. Together with Tear Fund, MOC organized and ran a two-week orientation course for short-term workers going overseas with various mission or development organizations.

The specialist trainers needed for the different courses included over 20 practising missionaries and other experts in their fields of knowledge. From 1978 to 1990 some 26 Missions made regular use of the MOC in the training of their missionaries and candidates, and over 1,100 people attended the courses. During this time, many Bible Colleges began to include similar courses into their own programme so that the unique contribution of the MOC was less needed. As Bulstrode had become increasingly crowded it was decided to close the MOC. There is a time and season for all things and the MOC had fulfilled its important role.

Operation World

Patrick Johnstone

Our early WEC leaders were passionate about gaining information that stimulated vision. In 1944 Norman Grubb asked Leslie Brierley to do a global survey for WEC. He was then working in Sierra Leone and Guinea-Bissau. This envisioned WEC in the post WW2 period and made WEC a truly global pioneer Mission. In 1959 Norman asked Leslie to take up research as a full time ministry based at the Highland Road HQ, thus the start of the International Research Office *(IRO)*. This led to Leslie's second great global survey - the **19 Point Programme for the Unevangelized**. This resulted in a new growth and advance for WEC into new countries and peoples.

I left the UK for Africa and service with the Dorothea Mission *(DM)* in 1962. The leader of the DM, Hans von Staden, had a passion for two things – evangelizing the growing slums of Southern Africa and prayer for world evangelisation. The latter was the focus of numerous Weeks of Prayer for the World in Africa and Europe. I made maps and gathered prayer information for these weeks, and then in 1964 was asked to write a booklet to give the prayer fuel. He suggested the title **Operation World.** This little booklet of 30 pages was so useful, I was asked to update it. I then said: "If I do this again, I ought to cover the other countries not covered in the first book!" I did not realize how complicated this would be.

I was then working in Rhodesia (now Zimbabwe) and it was a pariah nation under white minority rule, with strong trade sanctions imposed on it by the rest of the world. We had no suitable libraries for my research, and postal services were cut off with most of the world. This brought me into contact with Leslie Brierley in the new WEC HQ at Bulstrode. On furlough in 1969 I went to visit him - still bearing the wounds of the fatal car accident in which his wife Bessie had been killed. This started a relationship that changed my life, and, I believe the world.

Back in Rhodesia I needed help with contacting other countries for prayer information, so Leslie Brierley and his secretary, Violet Edson, became a postal service to pass on letters through Bulstrode. This enabled two global surveys to be completed for the next two Operation World books in 1972 and 1978. The latter went global with hundreds of thousands distributed.

This link led to Leslie Brierley approaching our then WEC leaders about asking me to become his successor as the International Research Secretary and to head up the IRO. Amazingly this was agreed and for the first and probably last time in WEC's history, a non-WECer was invited to be an elected international leader in WEC. Jill and I then moved with our three children to Bulstrode in 1980, which became my base for the next 22 years. It was a wonderful home for us as well as a base for global ministry within WEC. We spearheaded several major new advances in WEC and also published a further three editions of Operation World in 1985, 1993 and 2001.

Who can tell the impact on world evangelisation because of the IRO? Maybe a little list would help give a hint of this:

1. Two major growth and advance spurts in WEC generated by the STEP* Advance of 1984, and the RUN* initiative of 1996. The number of fields and WECers doubled. *(*see Glossary on p. viii)*

2. A total of over 2.5 million copies of OW in 16 languages distributed over the period 1978-2015. The royalties helping to both fund subsequent editions of OW, the costs of running the IRO and also purchasing the computer equipment to run the International Office. Some have said that this book was the most important missions book ever published in the 20th Century.

3. Over £100,000 worth of overhead transparencies marketed promoting world evangelization in the 1980s and 1990s.

4. A significant role in launching global prayer movements and the emergence of non-Western Missions - especially in South Korea, Brazil and among the Chinese.

5. Jill and Daphne's children's versions of OW are still selling well after 22 years. *(see illustrations opposite and p. 96)*

Praise God for the launch-pad for missions that Bulstrode became.

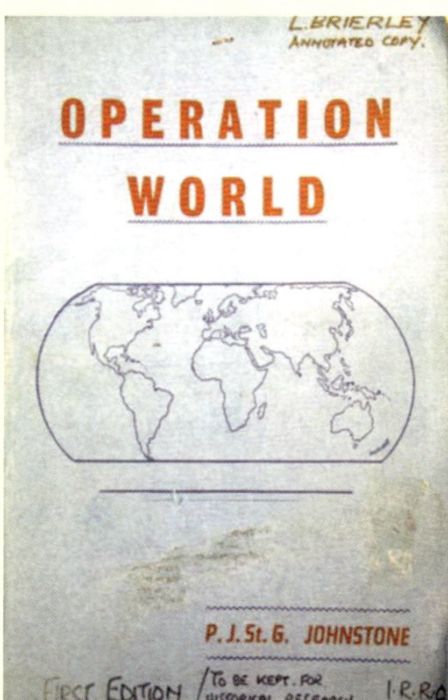

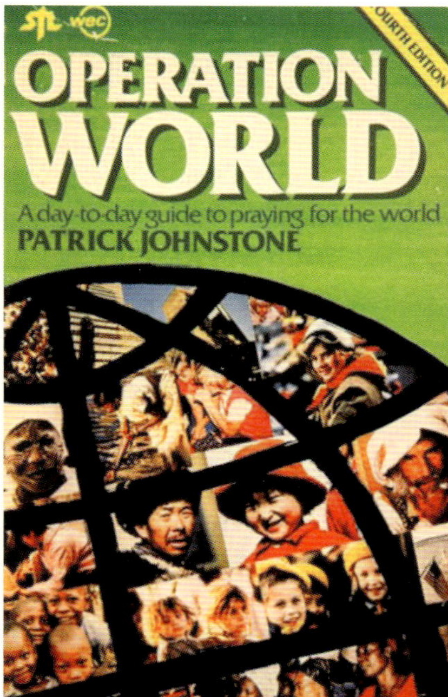

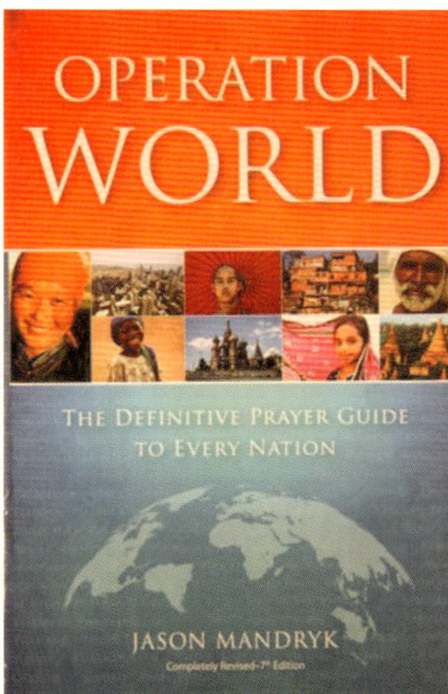

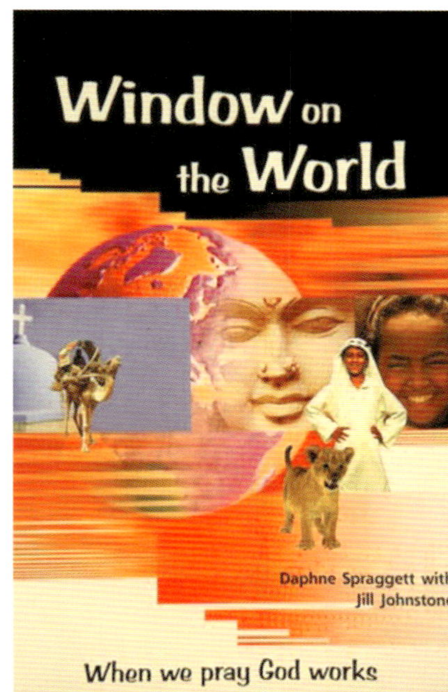

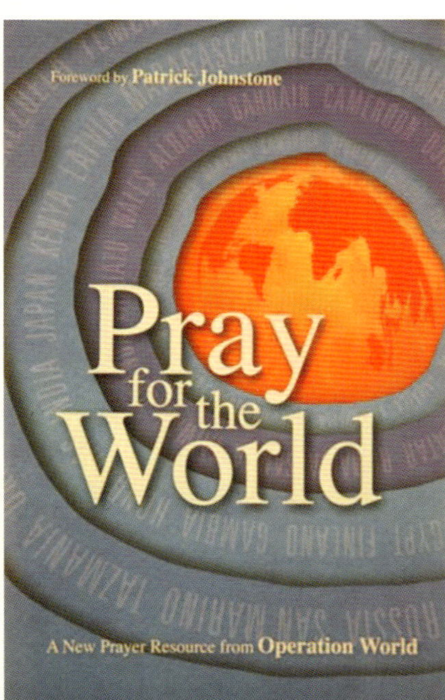

the front covers of different editions of ***Operation World****, which George Verwer refers to as "probably one of the most important missionary tools in the entire history of missions." above: the children's versions* ***You Can Change the World*** *and* ***Window on the World*** *left: the abridged version* ***Pray for the World*** *below: various different language versions of* ***Operation World***

I Grew up at Bulstrode

Sheena Wardrope

I moved to Bulstrode in the summer of 1967; I was eight years old and the house was to become my home for the next 14 years. I arrived with my parents and younger brother having driven down from the West Coast of Scotland. I remember feeling totally overwhelmed at the size of the place despite having previously lived in WEC's Bible College in Glasgow and then the Mission's Scottish conference centre, Kilcreggan House - both were large but nothing like Bulstrode.

A handful of people were already there when we arrived but we all lived in the flats, to the right of the entrance gates, as the house was the domain of the builders for a few weeks, or even months, before anyone could move in. I think we were the first family to actually move into Bulstrode once the first phase of renovation was completed and we lived in what is now the Verandah Lounge. I remember the buzz of excitement over the next few months with many more people arriving, in stages, as accommodation and offices were prepared. By then I was already settled in and proud to be able to show people round, though I got lost numerous times myself in the beginning - even looking for the nearest bathroom was an adventure!

Other very early memories include going down to the cellars in the Basement with my dad and discovering bedrooms (yes, I'm sure I remember correctly, there were bedrooms in the cellars!) with beds left unmade from the day the previous occupants left.

40 years between photos of Sheena by the Bulstrode swings
below: Sheena with her brother Martin and parents, Neil and Mary Rowe *photos: courtesy Sheena Wardrope*

The grounds were fun in those days with 75 acres of land and plenty of derelict out-buildings to explore. There were a few large tree-houses (complete with more mattresses left by the Bruderhof), a small log cabin, a two-roomed house (called the Swiss Cottage for some reason) that was completely studded with seashells and, by the swings that are still in use, there was an enormous metal maypole with four wooden handlebars on long chains. The children living at Bulstrode in those days had hours of great but rather dangerous entertainment. Sadly all these attractions had to be removed for health and safety reasons. Not only were they a potential danger, they attracted trespassers and, in the 60s, the occasional group of drug addicts. My dad had a moped in those days and made regular tours of the ground's perimeters to check all was well. One evening he came across a poacher, complete with a gun. Dad challenged him and said he was on private property. The poacher replied by asking who dad was. "I'm the property manager," he replied. "In that case," said the poacher, looking round at the rather overgrown section where they met, "you don't manage it very well do you!"

Growing up in an increasingly busy and inhabited Bulstrode was exciting but it wasn't what I would call a "normal family life." Although my parents provided a loving and stable base for my brother and me, we were often left to our own devices and attached ourselves to any of the many "uncles" and "aunts" (as we had to call WEC staff in those days) who could put up with us!

I hesitate to name names for fear of leaving people out, but there were some wonderful people who have left a life-long impression on me. I know they helped to "look after" me in terms of giving time and attention, but they were also a huge spiritual influence too. People like:

*Maria Baro *(see photo)* who opened up her home, or at least her room, to a group of young teenage WEC kids for Bible study, prayer, lots of laughter and occasionally some Cuban cooking!

*Jill Pressley (now Brierley) who read the Narnia series to Helen Gabriel and myself on Sunday afternoons and then took us out into the garden to act out some of the scenes complete with the "Beavers' Home" and the "Stone Table."

*Jim and Kit Hayter were volunteers who lived part time at Bulstrode for a few years and Kit took a real interest in me and my school friends. She often prepared a home-cooked, or should I say room-cooked, meal for my friends and was instrumental in one of them coming to the Lord.

*Jean Walker (she was especially good to have as a friend as she ran the tuck shop!) won't ever be forgotten. Among other responsibilities, she did the school runs. On the day of my Maths O level we had a bit of an argument as she dropped me off at Chalfonts College. I left for the exam in tears. Jean realised that this was not a good situation so rushed back to Bulstrode and interrupted the morning Chapel session to ask everyone to pray for me. I got an "A" in the exam, which was absolutely not expected even in the best circumstances! I guess it was an answer to prayer - and perhaps partly due to the result of Bill Elcock's patient endeavours to give me extra Maths tuition - and he is yet another person I shall always be thankful for.

I moved out of Bulstrode when I got married (the reception was held at Bulstrode) and I was more than ready to finally live in a "normal" house; in fact I confess it was one of the reasons I wanted to get married!

My associations with Bulstrode continue, however, as my husband has been a WEC UK trustee for several years. It is an interesting coincidence that my father, Neil Rowe, was instrumental in finding Bulstrode and taking on the management of the property in those early days and now my husband, also called Neil, has been involved in the momentous decisions made at the closing of the WEC/Bulstrode era.

above: Maria Baro (photo: Wendy Baldwin)

note: Mary Rowe wrote "Why on Earth a Mansion?" about WEC taking on Bulstrode (see p. 96)

above: Wedding Day for Neil and Sheena - main staircase at Bulstrode

below: 34 years between the photos taken underneath the Keep

Our Family Oasis

Shireen Ettrick

My first ever memory is a memory of Bulstrode. It is the 17th August 1970 - my fourth birthday. In front of me are two cakes - one vanilla-iced and one chocolate - and I am standing in the wooden playroom off the old Nursery.

This was actually my second time at Bulstrode; my first was in June 1968, aged not quite two years old, when my parents, Don and June Rowley, were visiting the UK after ten and a half years on the field. WEC must have just moved into the building, which my father describes in his diary as "a huge place and quite delightful." In 1970 he wrote: "So nice to see the green, the spacious rooms, and quiet, after the noise and cramping of town life. We were given a grand suite of rooms right over the main drive and the boys had a little room next to the tunnel, such as they had read about." The greenness, the quiet, the beauty and grandeur of Bulstrode, and that storybook quality of "tunnels," secret staircases and hidden doors are some of the aspects my family still love today.

Lost in Bulstrode

Arriving from hot, barren Central Asia, our eyes would be surfeited with the most intense green we had seen for two years, and as soon as we had put our suitcases down Miriam and Naomi would disappear, with the intention of getting "lost" and discovering some new feature of Bulstrode they had never seen before. Coming from a country run on suspicion and mistrust, where we had to escort our girls everywhere for their safety, we revelled in being able to allow them to roam freely, knowing that whomever they met, they would be treated with kindness and understanding. Once we lost Miriam when she was about five years old and found her walking happily along the corridor hand-in-hand with Stewart Moulds. Apparently she had entered the Moulds' flat uninvited, and now Stewart was returning her to us. Although it was a Sunday afternoon, Stewart wasn't irritated by the interruption, just amused at the way Miriam obviously felt at home. Our children still sense this affection from the Bulsrode residents and feel they are visiting close relatives.

When I was a child in Bulstrode, it was very different. We were sternly reminded that children mustn't run in the corridors and families with young children ate separately, in the Small Dining Room nicknamed the "Bawl Room" - I didn't get the pun till years later. The first time I was left alone in a bedroom near the Small Courtyard, aged seven, I became conscious of the empty darkness of the corridors and of how far away my parents must be. I screamed and screamed and screamed, until someone passing by heard me and called my mother.

But there were fascinating people like Jean who ran the Bulstrode shop, who could waggle her ears and lift her hat off her head by holding her nose and blowing. And Charlton Smith, a small, neat white-haired man whom I watched, spellbound, as he created collages of pictures and blocks of colour on the walls of what are now the White Stairs. My favourites were a picture of a boy with a puppy, next to a large chocolate Swiss roll, and a painting of silvery-white horses dashing out of a foaming sea. I could show you exactly where they were placed, even now.

I remember playing with the Freitag girls in the rubble in the Stables, and staining my clothes by rolling down the steep, grassy slopes of the field. We had barbecues on the lake shore and picked raspberries in the fields beside the drive. There were ginger nut biscuits at coffee time, but my father always carried Ahmed's Mango Pickle to enliven the "Bulstrode meals." And at Reception sat the awe-inspiring switchboard, with its beige, brown and cream switches, which I imagined myself flicking back and forth. How I loved the "bing-bong" of the intercom system and longed to say, just once, those familiar words: "Breakfast is ready. Breakfast is now being served in the Dining Room."

I also loved the long corridor with its squeaky linoleum and the names of all the countries WEC had entered, in chronological order, along the wall. I always looked for the one that mentioned "our" country, 1947, and knew that that was where my parents - and therefore my family - fitted into the story of WEC.

"...the greenness, the quiet, the beauty..."

Winifred Davies 27/5/67 *John Haywood 8/1/66* *Jim Rodger 25/11/64* *Ron Davies 26/10/47*
Bill McChesney 25/11/64 *Muriel Harman 25/11/64* *Cyril Taylor 25/11/64*

the photographs of WEC martyrs mentioned by Shireen - dates represent when they passed from active service into Glory

All around the walls of the Chapel, above the wooden panelling, was another visual aid which made a deep impression - a frieze of black and white photos of WECers who had died while on the field. As a new worker, my father had been expecting to work with one of them, Ron Davies, but Ron was among those martyred in the turbulence of Indian Partition in 1947, not long before my father set sail. "This is serious," the photos, names and dates said to me. "There *is* a cost ..."

At the end of our stay, my brothers Philip, Mark and I would bundle up the bedding for a favourite ritual: "bombing" our sheets, towels and pillowcases from the very top of the stairs far, far down to the bottom; we tried to see who could get all their laundry into the basket below, without it catching on the banisters or missing the target. Miriam and Naomi have carried on this tradition, adding scoring and a points system.

Outside, everyone would gather around our Landrover and pray for us before we drove off on our long journey to Pakistan - the gravel crunching under our wheels as it still does today - "sending us out" with a real sense of God's family, of solidarity and support.

As a new Candidate, in 1998, I got to know Bulstrode at a new level. I mistakenly thought I needed to "prove myself" to be a tough WECer and so I tried to do as many household duties as those without children. Tucking six-month old Miriam under one arm, carrying toys and fresh towels with the other, I climbed staircases and cleaned rooms I had never seen before. If Miriam was asleep, it was easier; I could sometimes leave her with Daphne Spraggett at Reception and Daphne would call me over the intercom when Miriam woke. The routine of wiping sinks, refilling supplies, changing tea-towels and vacuuming carpets gave me a lasting appreciation of all that is done to host guests. More unpleasant was trying to carry on phone conversations while sitting in a corridor with the telephone wire stretched around the corner so I could be near our bedroom door.

At first I felt let down by the ordinariness of WECers whom I considered to be spiritual giants, but as we lived with them in Bulstrode, I came to see that God is the Great One, working through these ordinary people. As I saw men in positions of great responsibility loading the dishwasher and heard respected leaders confessing wrong attitudes and asking forgiveness, I realised I didn't need to prove myself, but simply rely on Him.

I have a photo of Tim, little Miriam and myself standing underneath the archway of the great door of Bulstrode on 2nd September 1998, the day we left for Central Asia. My mother is looking away , but my father looks straight at the camera. He is not smiling and I, who know him, can easily read the lines of pain. This is my grandparents' sacrifice repeated; this is a picture of parents letting go of their children for the sake of God's Kingdom.

And so Bulstrode became our family's oasis, our place of rest. It was a decompression chamber in which we could acclimatise to England, or prepare our hearts after hectic furloughs to face the challenges of the field again. The Bulstrode staff had all the cost; we experienced only gain as we luxuriated in the compassion and complete understanding of the WEC family, in the beloved Children's Library, in Marmite and peanut-butter on toast, morning Chapel services, the beauty of the grounds and some much-needed space to seek God's presence.

"If Heaven is only a little bit like Bulstrode," said Naomi, "I'll be happy."

Appointment with God

Vivienne Ely

In 1978 Phil and I had been married for two years and enjoyed considerable affluence and frequent socialising, but during that year Phil had said to me on several occasions that he felt so happy with life he wanted to thank God for this gift. I do remember on one of these occasions he had suggested we go to church together that Sunday morning. My response was to hand him an alka seltzer from the bathroom cabinet, convinced he must be suffering from a bad hangover. Phil made no further attempts to change our Sunday practices.

In the December of the same year Phil's godmother and distant aunt had been invited to the HQ of a large missionary organisation called WEC in Gerrards Cross for their Christmas Open Evening, so she rang us insisting that we attend as well. It would have been the height of rudeness to refuse but on the actual evening, the Friday before Christmas, Phil was delayed at an important exhibition in London so I had to attend alone - with some dread in my heart to say the least! There was a young couple there that night of our age, missionaries working in Japan, who had spent the day fasting and praying asking the Lord for one person at the show to be changed by the events of the evening. The show was performed on the enormous stairway in the Reception area of Bulstrode. As I sat beside Aunt Barb watching the show I remember vividly one particular turn where Michael Ross-Watson, a missionary working in Indonesia, shared about his life there. As he spoke I saw his whole face light up with such a radiance and I knew that there was someone who was speaking just to me through him. It made me feel very uncomfortable and even afraid and yet in awe all in the same moment. Of course as soon as he left the stage I started to convince myself that it had been entirely in my imagination.

I knew that there was someone who was speaking just to me through him

As the performance came to an end, I made a hasty retreat in the hope of escaping, but as I headed for the door the young couple of our age, Gillian and Herman Spronk, stopped me in my tracks and invited me to join them for refreshments of tea and home made cakes. I didn't have the heart to refuse even though I was still feeling ill at ease with the performance. As we sat together, Gillian relayed her testimony of when and how she had become a Christian. She shared many things that had been wrong and sinful in her life and as she spoke I couldn't help but think that I too had done many of the same sins. But instead of admitting this to her I argued that she couldn't believe in the Bible, particularly with all the current knowledge of evolution. What I did not admit was that I had never read the Bible and I was coming to question a lot of the beliefs in evolution which I had studied intensively. I was extremely impressed with this new friend and when she told me about a very active church in the next village of Chalfont St Peter I promised her that night that I would go once during the Christmas period.

When I returned home that night to share with Phil that I had promised this girl that I would go once to Gold Hill Baptist church, he was delighted, insisting that he had wanted many times over the year to attend a church and thank God for his life and happiness.

The following Sunday, seats were reserved for us at the front by Aunt Barb's dear friend and confidante Iris Moules. Iris had been invited to our cottage on the Saturday and, trying to impress this dear saint with my somewhat bigoted views, I announced to her that HER GOD could never forgive Susan Atkins. Susan was a member of the Charles Manson commune, and had just been convicted of murdering Sharon Tate (Roman Polanski's wife), who was heavily pregnant when the brutal attack occurred. I had just read the book called *Helter Skelter* which was written by the prosecuting lawyer. As Iris sat doing her knitting in our cottage she told me that God had already forgiven her. During her stay in prison, as Susan Atkins awaited the sentence of the electric chair, the law was changed in the state of California from the death sentence to life imprisonment; in prison Susan had become a Christian and written a book called *Child of Satan, Child of God*. Iris gave me a copy of the book and needless to say God used this to have a very profound affect on my trust and belief in Him.

This was a more cherished event than even our marriage had been

That Sunday was the beginning of seven years of attendance at Gold Hill Baptist Church by both Phil and I. We were baptised together on the Easter Sunday morning of 1979 in the presence of both Iris and Aunt Barb. Very few of our family attended, being rather perplexed by our recent fervent church-going and unable to understand our desire for baptism when both of us had been through a christening service at birth. But for Phil and I, in our new found relationship with our Father and His Son, this was a much more cherished event than even our marriage had been.

During the Christmas WEC Open Evening of 1979 I gave my testimony on the stage and then in 1980 I produced the show basing the entire contents on the work and testimonies of the staff of WEC Press. Some years later Phil became very involved in the work of BETEL and visited their original centre in Spain. We both still remain very committed to this growing body of men and women whose lives have been saved from a broken existence of life-dominating addictions. From 2002 onwards we went on several short mission trips with WEC travelling to Mexico, Cambodia and South Korea. The main purpose of these trips was to teach the overseas WEC staff on the use of computers which were a fast growing, new technology. The last of these trips to Cambodia was in December 2006 where I was asked to teach English alongside the computer classes. I was unexpectedly made redundant from my long standing scientific job just before the trip, but in January 2007 I completed and passed my TEFL* certificate. From March 2007 until the Spring of 2014, I taught English to the yearly intake of foreign Volly Helpers at Bulstrode, some of whom went on to be missionaries with WEC. *(*Teaching English as a Foreign Language)*

This year Phil and I will celebrate our 40th Wedding Anniversary in June. That same month we will also attend the closing celebration of WEC Bulstrode after nearly 50 years of serving as the International Headquarters of WEC. Our walk with God over these last four decades has always involved us with WEC so it will be with sadness we anticipate this door closing in our lives. Or perhaps God in His infinite wisdom has other plans....

PART THREE

80s and 90s

Christmas Open Evening in the Bulstrode Entrance Hall, early 80s
photos: WEC archives

above: the Audio Visual Room in the Basement - more recently this room was used as the IT Office then for Management
inset: Iain at the controls below: Iain and Jane Fairweather (back row centre) with their Candidate group photos: I Fairweather

Beginnings and Growth of the Audio Visual Department

Iain Fairweather

It was on the Candidates' Course in 1976 that we felt led to set up a media department to promote WEC activities. We had both previously done courses with Radio Worldwide and had a keen interest in Cassettes Worldwide (an initiative set up by Leslie Brierley). In the autumn of 1976 we moved into a small room at the end of the Bulstrode Basement. We began producing cassette copies of meetings and experimenting with solar recharging systems and battery powered projectors for field use. In 1977 it was suggested we participate in a series of seminars on cassette ministries being run by Vigo Soggard in West Africa. We attended the week-long course in Kumasi, Ghana and then undertook a four-week field tour with a view to producing an audio-visual of WEC's work there.

On our return we produced an 80-slide audio-visual that was well received. In the autumn of 1977 it was proposed that we move to Glasgow to gain further experience working with Roy Spraggett. Apart from recording all the sessions of *Intercon '78* in Kilcreggan, and an AV on Portugal, the most significant project was *Edinburgh '80* which brought together a large number of Missionary Societies to review the Unreached Peoples, which had the slogan: **A Church for Every People by the Year 2000**.

In 1981 we returned to much larger facilities in the Bulstrode Basement to begin work with Patrick Johnstone on the **To Every People** audio-visual. At the time, it was an exciting new vision and throughout the 80s we produced over 1,200 copies of the slide/tape programme in 13 languages, including Korean, and it was used by numerous Missions around the world. Other AV programmes included **STEP - Strategy To Every People**, **A Visit to Spain** and **It's Your Move** which was converted to a promotional video for the *Mission '90 TEMA* Conference*. AVs on Senegal and Bourofaye School *(BCS)* were also produced.

**The European Missionary Alliance*

Apart from helping raise our three children, Jane's role at Bulstrode saw her involved in the Kitchen, hostessing visitors and in the early 90s working with Chris Scott as editor of the **Warrior Magazine** *(see below)*. I was also involved in the Field Committee, the Finance Committee, Candidates' Committee and for a time headed up Extension Ministries*. Around this time in the AV Deptartment, it became clear that video was the way forward and basic equipment was used to produce videos on Senegal, BCS and The Gambia. There was also a short video on **The Gateway Peoples**. But in those days, video and computer editing equipment was very expensive and the demand for AV programmes dried up and led to the demise of the AV Department. *(*department for WEC events, materials etc)*

It is easy to get nostalgic looking back but there were some great times, some difficult times but overall, very fulfilling times. The children all have happy memories of growing up in Bulstrode.

above: Iain took many photos of and designed prayer cards for WEC missionaries before they embarked for the field - this example is of the editor and his family in 1992 before they left for Spain - the photo was taken near the Lily Pond

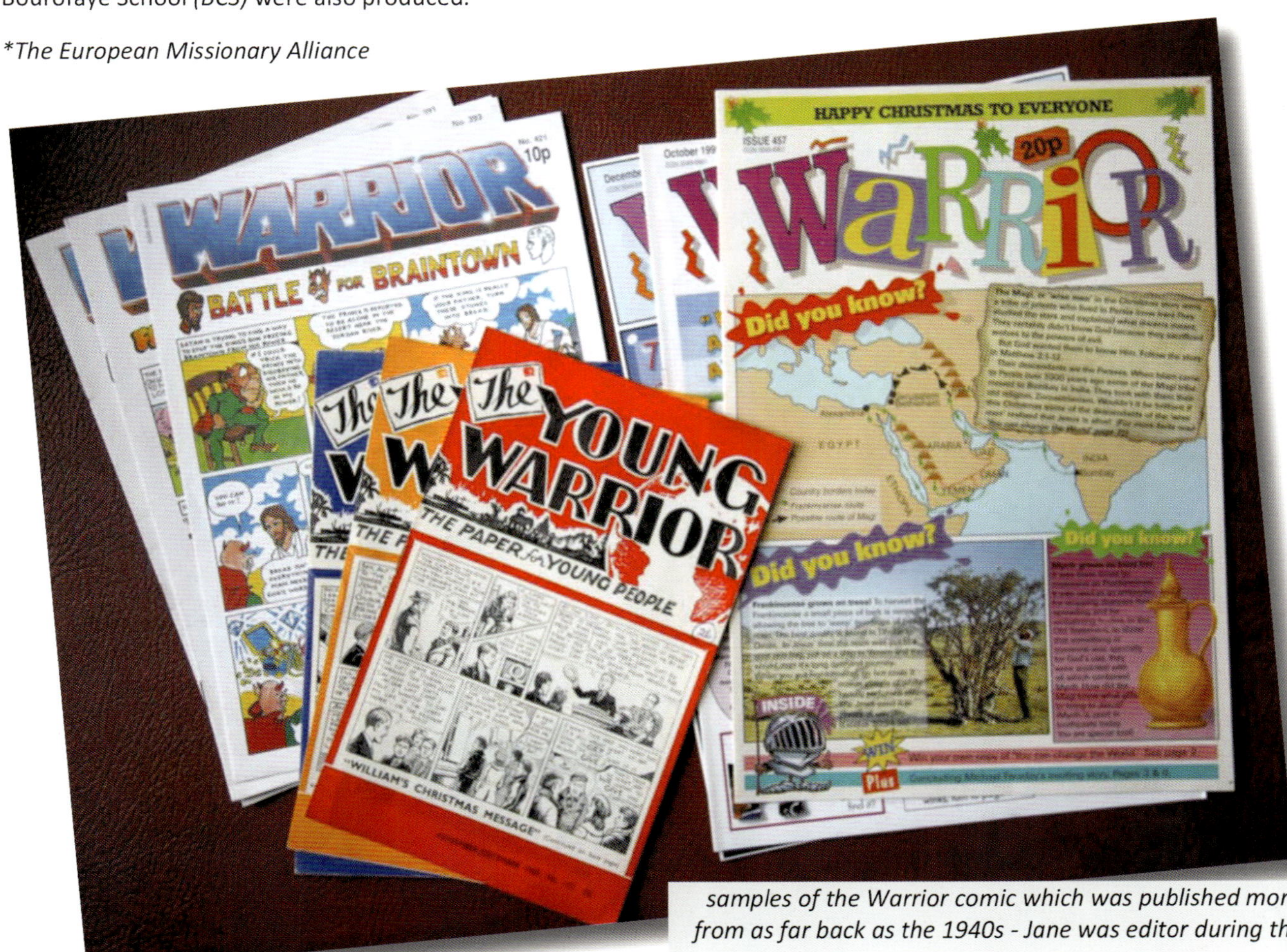

samples of the Warrior comic which was published monthly from as far back as the 1940s - Jane was editor during the 90s

Rabbits and Bonfires **Francis Blackmore**

Run Rabbit Run Run Run

During my stint as Estate Manager from 1979 - 1983, one of the projects that I did was to grow vegetables and fruit for the large Bulstrode household. Unfortunately we had quite a plague of rabbits at that time and they often got to the veggies before us! So I acquired a 12 bore shotgun - and a license of course.

There was a German family, Rudi and Renate Lutgarth and children, staying at Bulstrode to improve their English before going on to The Gambia field. Rudi had a left-hand drive car which enabled us to go out in the evening, dazzling the rabbits with the headlights and I would fire the gun out of the window. What was also very useful was that Rudi was excellent at skinning and preparing the rabbits for the barbeque.

On a pleasant summer's evening, just as it was getting dark, we drove through the Inner Courtyard to go down on to the south lawns and do a sweep across and down to the little valley. As we drove through the archway, a young lady visiting from the USA saw us drive through with my shotgun sticking out of the front window.

As Rudi and I cruised slowly around the south lawns we were mystified why there were no rabbits – normally we would see dozens! We then went back and up the Lime Avenue and around the back of the Long Water, still not seeing any rabbits. Coming around the end of the lake we found a log had been put across the track. We stopped and suddenly out jumped Brian Cripps and Mike McKenzie from behind a tree exclaiming: "Oh, it's you! We have called the police."

The young American lady, on seeing us with the gun, had run to Reception and told them what she had seen, not knowing who I was. While we were driving around the lawns, unbeknown to us, there were about ten people following us, hence the reason for no rabbits. Apparently when we stopped, the group stopped at a safe distance. When we reversed, they reversed even quicker. So that night the rabbits were spared!

The Chequered History of a May Day Rubbish Bin

One day when having a general tidy up in the Press Yard, I came across a 45 gallon drum of TVO (tractor vaporising oil*). The drum was nearly empty but it had been left there for so long that the opening was completely rusted up and immovable.

*(*TVO is a cross between petrol and paraffin; when heated it becomes very inflammable like petrol, but when cold it burns very poorly).*

Francis, back in those days of flared trousers; in the picture below he is driving the tractor *photos: WEC archives*

I always enjoyed a bonfire and often had one, especially during the winter months, burning scrub and prunings etc. So I said to two Bulstrode teenagers: "Let's have some fun." We took the drum up to a bonfire that I had burning, well away from the house and people, near the Long Water. We placed the drum on the fire and retreated to a safe distance, behind a heap of soil. Nothing happened for a while - the drum was made of a good heavy gauge metal - but then we heard slight popping sounds and we could see the end of the drum starting to bulge out. All of a sudden a great blue flame, about 30 feet in length, shot out of the end of the drum together with a very loud hissing sound and the drum flew off in the opposite direction to the flame, into the woods! When it had cooled down we retrieved it; the end had come cleanly off, and it made a perfect bin for use on May Day.

Around the Campfire

One of the blessings of looking after the grounds in the early 80s was having many Voluntary Helpers working with me. There were some who stayed at Bulstrode for as long as a year and I got to know them very well.

Often in the winter time if we were working in the further parts of the estate, instead of coming in for the coffee break we would take a flask of coffee and biscuits with us. This would save all the time of taking off wet and muddy boots etc.

During the coffee time we would sit around a nice warm fire and discuss anything from international affairs or British social history to something that was shared in the morning Chapel time. We had a flow of missionaries coming through Bulstrode and many were an inspiration to hear and meet, and they often impacted these young people's lives.

Some years later in '93 and '96 I was part of the team manning the WEC exhibition at the large Youth Mission Conference in The Netherlands. At least six people came up to me and introduced themselves by saying, "Do you remember me?" They said how their time at Bulstrode had been so important in their lives and several were now on the mission field. Even two or three remembered our fireside discussions!

Bulstrode Wildlife

The delightful cartoons on this page were the work of Connie Lyne, who joined WEC in the 1950s. They reflect something of Bulstrode life in the early 1980s, when Francis Blackmore (that's him welcoming the little guests) was Estate Manager.

As Pauline Brogden points out in her article on the Bulstrode Kitchen *(p. 50)*, much of the produce was home-grown. The cartoon below depicts the constant battle against the bunnies, alluded to in Francis's night-time hunting story.

In more recent times, Bulstrode residents have made use of private allotments, but the little "consumers" continue to make their trips to the supermarket!

The pigeon cartoon below depicts Neil Rowe heading up the Lime Walk. Neil - featured in Sheena's article *(p. 38)* - held various roles at Bulstrode, including UK Director and Bulstrode Manager.

Pigeons and rabbits have not been the only wildlife observed in the Bulstrode grounds. In our time, Rose and I have seen:

*deer (roe and muntjac) gracefully leaping the fence - and we have also heard them raucously barking during the mating season.

*foxes, bushy-tailed and flame-red against the pristine snow.

*squirrels galore - I know at least one Manager who made a valiant attempt to reduce their number with a shot-gun.

*Canada geese rearing a family of goslings on the Lily Pond island. The shot-gun came out again prior to GOFest to make the grass accessible for walking.

*many varieties of birdlife, including red kites, green woodpeckers, jays (the distinctive flash of blue can often be seen near the bend in the driveway), parrots, song thrushes (one avid singer frequents a tree at the head of the Beauty Walk in summer), herons by the ponds and the raucous rooks and crows in the tops of the lime trees (dining on mistletoe I presume).

*there are families of badgers too at the top of the Lime Walk - Rose has seen the streak of black and white and heard the snuffling at dusk.

*moles - never seen, but they leave their mountainous marks all over the park. Another Manager went hunting them too.

Bulstrode is home to a host of residents!

The Youth Department

Paul Round

Paul and Lynne Round are Bulstrode's longest-serving residents having lived here from 1989 to the present day. Paul, WEC's Youth Coordinator during that time, records his memories:

*A warm, dry, dusty cellar, with piles of tent sacks covered in layers of brick dust, put to bed each autumn and woken again each spring - some to be used on May Day.

*The excited chatter of young people enthused and full of energy, while older regulars sit in the corner reminiscing, all here for pre-Camp training.

*Small youth groups, some occasionally camping in the grounds and more recently the buzz of **Warrior** and **Teen Camp** reunions in full swing. *(Camps are run each Summer for several weeks in seaside locations - Warrior Camp is for 9-13 year-olds, while Teen Camp caters for 14-17 year-olds).*

*Back in 1989 a Youth Ministry was reborn; Bulstrode became the base to launch **World Adventure** weekend programmes for all ages as well as being a hub for the **Camps**.

*For me the memories are primarily of people, a team of six at one point and many more involved in "Youth" activities (the list of people is too long to name).

***The Studio** as it was once known, a creative hub of ideas, possibilities - some wild, others to bear fruit in due season.

* Moving on brings mixed emotions for those of us involved in the Youth Ministry. In part, an unfulfilled vision, a lost dream, yet grateful for many lives challenged and changed. Bulstrode, with its grandeur as a former stately home, has seen the splendour of God at work and we have so much to thank Him for.

Personal Thoughts

Paul Round

From New Year house parties run by Chris Scott in the early 1970s, through coming to plan Camps and repair tents while still teaching on the Wirral, to becoming a resident staff member, raising a family and developing a ministry, my Bulstrode road has been long and varied.

Not many remember opening the front gate at 6.30am for the milk man, who would leave up to 8 or 9 crates of milk in bottles outside if we'd overslept. Unlocking all the doors was a duty in those days too as well as "lock up." The family friendly Christmas parties in the Reception Area by the Christmas tree and the meal and entertainment for all those who came to help us from the local area added to the strong family feel of our early days here.

Bulstrode and its grounds have provided a great place for the family to grow up in. Living in the biggest house in Gerrards Cross with all its character has been a privilege - and the envy of some school friends, while youngsters here sometimes envied the big houses of their friends.

But by far the greater privilege has been to see God at work in providing for our own needs and the needs of the Mission, as well as being involved in the spiritual journeys of so many people. Candidates, Short Term workers, Mission and Me* participants, Camp folk and many, many more have passed through this place, met God and never been the same since. Lynne and I give praise and thanks to God. *(*Lynne coordinated this for many years)*

opposite: camp equipment stored in the Bulstrode Basement
below: aerial view of Camp at Cromer - Warrior in the large field, Teen in the foreground *photos: courtesy WEC Camps*

Journey into WEC

Adam Lowe

Adam and Nicola (right) are part of the WEC Short Term Team. Here Adam shares his story:

Camp was a hugely influential part of my journey into WEC. Attending the Camps as a camper gave me a spiritual lift each year whilst also reminding me that God is working in a world outside of my own.

However, attending as a leader has impacted me more for a number of reasons. It was at Camp where I met my wife. As we journeyed into missions together we maintained our connection with Camps, going back year on year.

Now I'm a member of the Camps' Leadership Team shaping the future of WEC Camps. It has been so encouraging to see young people taking the same first steps that I took at their age.

photo: courtesy A Lowe

Impact of Camp

Kate Newhook

When I was 15 my friend at school invited me to go on a WEC Camp with her during the summer holidays with the church she attended. I didn't really know what to expect and when we arrived I didn't like the set up, but during the week I began to enjoy the meetings and activities more, as well as making friends. Towards the end of the week, I decided that I wanted to start a relationship with the Jesus that I had been hearing about every day and so I began my journey of faith.

Kate is now Children's and Youth Worker at Farnham and Hedgerley Community Church

The WEC Family

Olive Howard

Now in her eighties, Olive (right, centre, in white) is as busy and active as ever. Just one of her roles is to organise the WEC relatives' day, when parents and relatives of WECers, such as those pictured with her, visit Bulstrode and enjoy fellowship. The article below first appeared about 25 years ago in the WEC Press publication "Bulstrode - the Home of WEC International."

Olive Howard sailed for Côte d'Ivoire, West Africa, in 1958. She is a Bible translator and co-ordinated the Gban New Testament Project. Her home church is Upney Baptist, Barking in Essex.

The WEC family has been special to me right from my early Candidate days at our former Headquarters. Now we are at Bulstrode, the sense of family seems heightened.

When I'm in Africa, Bulstrode is a lifeline for prayer, for monthly finances, for newsy reports, and is a safe place to store our back-up disks of the translation, as well as a couple of trunks in the Basement. Arriving in the UK, I feel the warmth of the welcome. At Bulstrode there is:

*a car to meet me at the airport

*always a room when needed (or at least a bed!)

*time given me by our leaders from their busy lives for hospitality and a personal chat

There's renewing here for body, mind and spirit:

*quiet walks through the gardens and grounds

*ministry in daily Chapel times

*courses to sharpen my skills (for example, a Church Growth course, and an introduction to *Windows 95*)

*I can even renew my wardrobe down in the Boutique!

There are resources and help available to me:

*is it a mosquito net or a solar lantern I need? Then Unimatco can supply it. *(see p. 53)*

*am I looking for ideas for a presentation, information, tranparencies or leaflets as I prepare for meetings? The Extension Office, the IRO *(International Research Office)* and the Youth Department are ready to share their expertise and provide materials.

*what about the series of new readers' booklets we are planning? Over the years WEC Press has worked with us to print and publish Gban Scripture portions, reading books and hymn books.

More importantly, being here at Bulstrode stretches and sharpens my global vision. I meet up with people from all over the world, hear about and pray for what's happening "out there" beyond the limits and concerns of my own corner in Côte d'Ivoire.

So I thank God for Bulstrode and the Bulstrode family who are working together with us to make Christ known worldwide.

The Bulstrode Kitchen 1985-2000

Pauline Brogden

"Trust the Lord for £1,000 to give you a buffer for the catering account" - wise words from an experienced WECer as I became responsible for the Bulstrode catering. Within a few weeks God had provided it in amazing ways.

Mike and I joined WEC knowing our gifts were to enable people to "reach the unreached", so it was my joy and privilege (most of the time!) to serve all who passed through the Dining Room, from Candidates to Coordinating Council members. Our team of 3 or 4, including 2 Vollies, had good times together cooking for 80 people each day, with numbers doubling at Conference time. At 11.30am each day we took time to read God's Word and pray together; we chatted and encouraged each other as we worked.

At the beginning, most of the vegetables were grown in the walled garden - picked at 8.00am and on the table by 1.00pm. Autumn yielded plums in abundance, which we froze for winter or even exchanged for other produce from our supplier. Candidates helped to harvest the potatoes; and who can forget the green beans, cabbages, parsnips, peppers, tomatoes and aubergines grown by Don Eckford?

Here are some of the highlights:

1. Getting to know almost every UK WECer and others from around the world as we ate together in the Dining Room.

2. Teaching and encouraging Vollies with their culinary skills and in their walk with Jesus.

3. Catering for happy weddings and poignant funerals or thanksgiving services.

4. Experiencing the generosity of God and His people sending gifts of food and money.

Of course there were challenges. Anyone in catering will tell you it is a demanding job. Food can be an emotive subject and you cannot please everybody all the time.

There were other challenges too - some personal, some family, but those years were some of the happiest and most fulfilling, as Mike and I helped to "reach the unreached" serving at Bulstrode.

the fruitful Bulstrode grounds - one job for the Candidates was to harvest the crops, particularly during the 80s and 90s

left: cartoon by Connie Lyne of Bulstrode residents sprinting up for second helpings

God Was Surely with Us

Jenny Webster (née Antill)

I have fond memories of Bulstrode and the more I think the more there are. We first arrived in 1984. I was just turning 8 years old and coming from a 3-bed semi in a Leicester suburb, to see the house appearing up the top of the long drive, was just the beginning of an adventure. All those people and all that history and space meant Bulstrode was the place of things to remember.

I remember the climb up into the ancient Keep *(right)* to play table tennis, avoiding the doves and pigeons, and climbing down to the smell of the cellars and the pool room, next to the amazing second hand treasure trove of 80s batwing jumpers and a matching tartan waistcoat and skirt for Sunday best. The smell of the tents that needed mending for the next summer's camp and the smell of the Laundry Room and rows of clothes flattening out in the heat.

Then of course, as we were the Bulstrode kids, there was the trip to school in the big red minibus with Jim. So many trees in the grounds meant an abundance of conkers and I remember a winner I beat Tim Johnstone with. I remember the anticipation of queuing up with the new BT "phone cards" under the stairs to speak to relatives, the little Children's Library of books, being told off by Tammam for running in the corridors, and a particular occasion when Hans caught us sliding down the orange ramp beside his staircase - what else was it for?!

And then there were the heroes. Starting with the corridor filled with those who had "gone before" and a tribute to the great CT Studd. There was a children's prayer meeting led by the wonderful late Jill Johnstone where we prayed for PM John and Sheila Kilkenny and learnt that we too could change the world through prayer. We met Aunty Heather who taught us *Diola** before we got to Senegal, Aunty Anne Greaves who would soon be our teacher, families from Korea, the USA, Canada and Europe who worked in all corners of the globe and who all had a passion for the gospel. *(*local tribal language in Senegal)*

below: the ramp beside the orange stairs, worn smooth not by suitcase wheels but by countless children's bottoms

There is plenty more to tell, of learning to ride my bike down the sheep track, the cold winter which literally brought in tons of snow, ice skating on the duck pond, rounders and volleyball on the lawns and the pet cemetery. We remember a consistent welcome from the likes of Jill and Howard Sayers and the Nicholas family, and the kindness of other WECers sending us on a trip to a Wimpy burger bar.

I don't go back often now but I will miss it. Sunburnt or washed out, with all the other MKs *(Missionary Kids)* on Mayday; extra hard boiled eggs and spam for Sunday tea; the only place my dad would ever harvest mistletoe or Uncle Iain Williamson would have to lock geese up at night. Like a crazy random family in transition but preparation for something bigger.

And I suppose that's what we are, a crazy mixed-together bunch, all part of God's wonderful worldwide family preparing for a better place. So when our paths cross again years later at some unexpected place at an unexpected time, if we've arranged it just for fun, or when we get to the other side, people who knew Bulstrode will give each other a knowing look. The conversation will carry on with something like "Do you remember when...?" and we'll understand the uniqueness and privilege it was to be part of the WEC and Bulstrode family, what a special place it was and we'll remember that **God was surely with us.**

God Answers Prayer - even in Backroom Offices

Mike Brogden

God used my desire to help Him with my legal background to "reach the unreached" by planting me in the Overseas Business Office *(OBO)* for my first four years, occupied with a job I had no idea about - booking travel for WEC workers to destinations I did not know via routes I had never heard of. It was an excellent lesson in learning that God did not actually need me after all. Gradually He got me used to the likes of Ouagadougou, Nyankunde, Nebobongo, Yaounde, Chiangmai, Phnom Penh, and good old Senegal which had only previously been a name in my stamp-collecting days. Why "good old" Senegal? Because we seemed to be forever sending workers there. One year, so many were going at the same time that it felt like we could have chartered a plane, just for the WECers.

The other side of OBO work was locating and sending out stuff which the fields needed but could not get locally. The very first request was for snake serum for Ghana... as if the like was handily available in leafy South Bucks! Oh, me of little faith... it turned out it was - from a scientific lab place near Heathrow airport. John and Brenda Chudley were my Godsend in finding most of the stuff needed by the fields in the late 1980s and through the 90s, from the simple mosquito and sand fly nets ... to the Katadyn water filters ... to the Toyota car parts ... to the computer bits and pieces (where they had superseded electric typewriters) ... to the carbon typewriter ribbons (where they hadn't) ... to the annual schools' equipment shipments for the MK schools at Vavoua and Bourofaye...and so on. The OBO couldn't have functioned without the Chudleys' Unimatco missionary procurement business in the Bulstrode Warehouse. *(see opposite)*

The UK Administrator's Office had been formed in 1978, with Jock Freitag as Administrator and Secretary to the Trustees. A dozen years later, he invited me to become his assistant. To some that might have felt like a bit of a poisoned chalice, for the first jobs he passed to me were the community charge or poll tax (remember the London riots?), income tax, national insurance and data protection. A year later, Jock and Mamie moved overseas to take up leadership of the Portugal field, Jock handing over to Noel Gibson temporarily - what would WEC have done without people like Noel and Zena, always willing to fill the gaps? - before the role was passed to me.

below: Unimatco packing boxes and a list of items for overseas

God always answers prayer - even in offices with backroom roles.

*I remember Singaporeans Patrick and Gina Lim's time on Autumn CO with UK visas up till December and us together booking in faith their onward flights to Brazil at Christmas when they still had no Brazilian visas, still had to pass medicals (including X-rays) at the Brazilian Embassy, and had to be out of the UK by Christmas! It all worked out.

*I remember praying with Pat Holdaway urgently returning from Africa to her sick relative in New Zealand, and waiting in faith with Pat, phone in hand, whilst the travel agent found the only remaining seat on the plane.

*I remember having to tell a Brazilian WECer on English language study in Brighton that, "No, he was not to give up and go home to his mother in four days' time."

*I remember telling another (also Brazilian) WECer that he must get on that plane at Amsterdam airport that was leaving for Senegal in ten minutes' time. (Both are fine, godly men serving the Lord today).

*I remember the British Home Office Minister (Anne Widdecombe) specifically changing the Immigration Rules to authorise Brad Parker to come from Australia as WEC UK Finance Director - a change in law which I believe still stands for all Missions today.

*I remember - with Radio Worldwide *(RW)* - trusting God for the acquisition of Barnardo's former "Naughty Girls" school in Rothwell as the new centre for all RW ministry at a time when Barnardo's had already accepted another offer ahead of ours, and yet seeing RW families move into the area in faith anyway, convincing even the selling agent that WEC would get the property.

It was great to be a part of that historic WEC faith story in the life of the RW team. May we who share the amazing privilege of being WEC from generation to generation never lose that spark of practical, outlandish, outworked faith which is the hallmark of resurrection life in the living God.

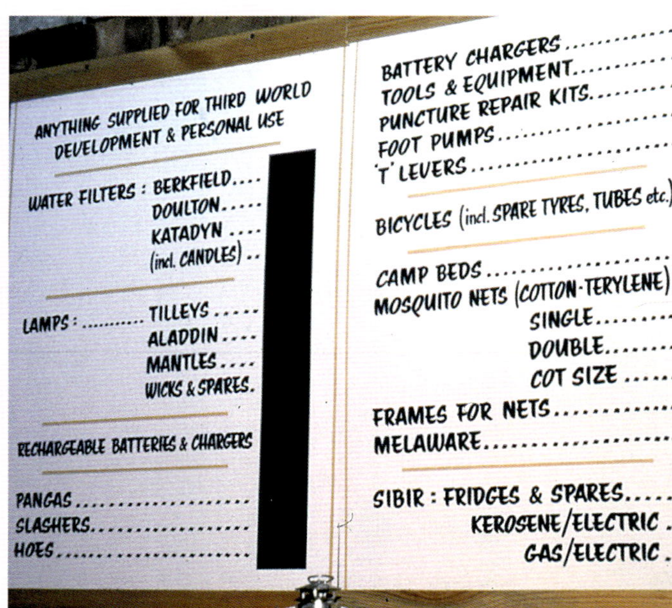

Unimatco

Anyone visiting Bulstrode from the 1980s through till 2008 might have been forgiven for thinking they had come to a second-hand Landrover shop. Several in a row were often parked on the grass or in the back yard. Along with other vehicles and countless other bits of machinery and equipment, these were destined for faraway places where they would be put to vital use by missionaries or national Churches who had requested them.

John and Brenda Chudley registered **Unimatco** *(the Universal Machine Transfer Company)* in 1977, having visited various countries in Africa and been challenged by the growing need for a ministry that could supply people on the front line with equipment not available "out there." In the early years they ran the company from their home in Chalfont St Peter, and then from a depot in Tatling End. During this phase WEC gave permission for them to use a workshop at Bulstrode along with a yard for storage space and for packing large containers.

In May of 1995 the whole firm moved to Bulstrode, where Unimatco took over use of the spacious Warehouse. WEC acquired planning permission for the small cottage by the back gate to be used for offices, so it was from there that Brenda handled the complex paperwork. The Chudleys also ran **Cedars** *(Charity Equipment for Development and Relief Services Ltd)*, providing equipment often free of charge.

As Mike Brogden points out in his article opposite, there was no limit to what Unimatco might send to foreign parts. Here are a few more examples of the type of things that found their way from Bulstrode to distant places:

*all manner of vehicles, including renovated Landrovers, ambulances, lorries

*cement mixers
*steel and wood for boats for the Sudan
*mosquito nets
*prosthetic limbs for victims of land mines
*37,500 garden hoes for Uganda and Zaire *(now the Democratic Republic of Congo)*
*live goats for breeding purposes in Tanzania

The ministry eventually had to cease due to Brenda's ill health, but not before thousands upon thousands of vital pieces of equipment, large and small, had been lovingly prepared and sent from Bulstrode's grounds to help and bless others.

top left: John and Brenda with truck

Grateful thanks to Barbara Birch (John's sister) and Janet Stewart (Brenda's sister) for help with this article

photos on these two pages courtesy Unimatco archives

Heather's Hilarious Wedding

Heather Donnelly

25th November 1989...
...was an exciting, hilarious day for the wedding of Alex Donnelly and Heather Grove. The actual service was at Gold Hill Baptist Church, but the rest of the day was at Bulstrode. As you can see, the "Bulstrode Mafia" were on duty and the flags of Uruguay and Senegal were visible in several places. Yodelling, sketches and the famous Patrick and Jill Johnstone acting as "Alex and Heather" stole the show with their singing act.

Photo 1: Arriving safely courtesy of the Bulstrode Mafia
Photo 2: The Bulstrode Mafia - the faithful chauffeurs (Colin Nicholas and Jim McWhinnie)
Photo 3: The newly married couple at the Entrance of Bulstrode (Uruguay and Senegal flags behind them)
Photo 4: Striding in eagerly for the marriage banquet (notice the very shiny floor)
Photo 5: Who is impersonating whom? Patrick and Jill Johnstone doing an "Alex and Heather" act at the wedding *photos: courtesy Heather Donnelly*

Bulstrode Boys

Brian and Daphne Cross

Bulstrode Boys 1996

Duties

For Bulstrode residents, duties and rotas were a daily part of life at Bulstrode and essential to the smooth running and maintenance of the Headquarters. The notice board was read like a newspaper to keep us up-to-date with our responsibilities as well as news from within the Mission. The duties ranged from washing-up to peeling potatoes, emptying bins, driving the Bulstrode minibus, locking up the premises at night (and unlocking in the morning), through to Reception duties which included manning the telephone switchboard and operating the Public Address system. Daphne has one early memory of being on Reception duty when Howard Sayers was in hospital for a few days and he rang in to speak to his wife Jill. At the flick of a switch Daphne put him through, but immediately realised she had connected him to the wrong Jill! As she interrupted the call in order to correct her mistake she heard Howard saying, "Hello darling," and Jill Johnstone replying, "You can't be my darling because my darling is sitting here next to me!" Embarrassing!

Bulstrode Boys

At the age of seven, our son Nathan, along with some of his WEC friends, took an interest in football (much to Brian's delight). This led to Brian giving them weekly football training sessions in the Bulstrode grounds which provided an ideal setting. The numbers grew rapidly as they invited their school friends and at one point we had 30 children. He was grateful for the help of Paul Round from WEC Youth and thankfully, the numbers levelled off to a manageable group of around 12-16 each week. With Paul's help and others, we even had a football camp. The boys stayed overnight in WEC Youth tents, followed by a training work-out in the morning and a trip to a Premier league match in London in the afternoon.

As they progressed, the boys were keen to play other teams so we entered six-a-side competitions in the local area. They were usually held over bank holiday weekends but most regular youth football was played on Sunday mornings, which we were keen to avoid. However, around this time a Christian league was started with churches participating from within a 15-mile radius of Bulstrode, and the games being played on Saturday mornings. This was ideal for us and over a seven-year period, the Bulstrode Boys had great success and won the League and Cup double on three occasions!

Our Christian witness through the football training was very low-key, and by example, but there was also a lot of relationship-building going on with the parents as well as the boys. Although at the time we didn't see any spiritual fruit from this work, several years after leaving Bulstrode, we were amazed to hear that one of the non-Christian boys who played in our team, had become a Christian. We eventually managed to meet up with him and hear his story. He became a Christian at university through the witness of a friend and he shared that his openness to this witness came about as a result of being impressed that both teams stood together before the start of every game while one of the managers prayed. Not only that, his mother also became a Christian through his witness to her. Seed sown does bear fruit eventually! Now that the boys are all in their late twenties/early thirties, we have been overwhelmed by appreciation from a number of them for the blessing it was to be part of the Bulstrode Boys football team.

photos: Brian Cross

Bulstrode Boys 1999

WEC Press

Brian and Daphne Cross

The motto for WEC Press was: "To enlighten men's eyes... we print."

WEC Press Team - early 90s photo: WEC Press
back row: John Tromans, David Carruthers, Ralph Hyde, Konrad Sparks, Hans Willems, Ron Harper
front row: Anne Tromans, Pauline Carruthers, Marie Harper, Daphne Cross, Brian Cross

Based on Ephesians 1:18, this motto was an inspirational factor in our commitment to what was basically, a backroom ministry. Producing "ammunition" for the troops (missionaries) on the frontline is another way of describing this ministry. The Word of God is described as being sharper than any two-edged sword and is able to judge the thoughts and attitudes of the heart *(Hebrews 4:12)*. In that case, a tract could be like a "bullet" and a Bible could be like a "nuclear bomb"! When the Bible changes the heart of someone like Billy Graham or David Yonggi Cho, it is not difficult to see the impact that the printed Word of God can have on a town, city or nation. As one of our printers put it: "My printing press is my pulpit."

Although literature is complimentary to missionary work, it can have a unique role in situations where conventional missionary work is restricted. Literature doesn't need a visa, doesn't need feeding, doesn't need electricity, doesn't need a rest and it can be read at any time of the day or night!

Much of our work involved designing and producing colourful, attractive and promotional literature for WEC in the UK, which included the bi-monthly magazine, *Worldwide*. About one third of our work went overseas, mainly to Africa, in places such as Burkina Faso, DR Congo (formerly Zaire), Senegal, Côte d'Ivoire, Liberia, Guinea-Bissau and The Gambia. To these countries we sent a mixture of literature which included reading primers, hymn books, Gospels, tracts, and New Testaments in a variety of languages. However, we also printed literature for Central Asia, and when Eastern Europe opened up, we printed tens of thousands of Gospels, particularly for Romania.

We were involved in a number of projects producing New Testaments or parts of the Bible in languages for the very first time. One such project was the Gospel of Matthew for the Tuareg people in Niger, Africa – it was printed on plastic paper to make it termite proof!

We also helped to set up printing workshops in Ghana and Nigeria by sourcing equipment and providing training at WEC Press and on site with the delivery of the equipment.

This was evangelism at a distance but one day in Heaven, we will discover how many mens' eyes we have enlightened.

Learning to Live in His Strength

Pauline Carruthers

April 1990. We sat in the car, halfway up the Bulstrode driveway – and prayed. Leaving family and friends and the security of our home was a huge leap of faith. Yet we were very much aware that the Lord had blessed us with enough faith to take that step into an unknown situation. We had no doubts regarding God's will or His call to serve Him within WEC Press, but just for a moment, the magnitude of the mansion and surrounding grounds and the uncertainty of our ability to cope with such an incredible change of lifestyle seemed overwhelming.

Adjusting to life in a tiny flat in close proximity to three other families was, for me, the hardest part of life in the Mission HQ. Yet giving it to Jesus day by day brought joy and an incredible appreciation of the lovely surroundings – the stunning aroma of the flowering lime trees and the glorious Beauty Walk *(below)*, where the bluebells, azaleas and rhododendrons highlighted the onset of springtime. Precious fellowship with our nearest neighbours richly blessed us, as did the "coffee and chat" times in the garden with other friends and the Voluntary Helpers.

The Lord enabled us all to integrate well into the structure of the Mission HQ, adjusting to the daily routine of life with rotas for Reception, weekend duty and so on. Routine became normal as did learning to live more frugally! Prayer became spontaneous as needs arose. The weekly Prayer Meeting and monthly Prayer Days were always a blessing, though there were times when we were tempted to take time out. Busy-ness alongside family responsibilities could occasionally overwhelm. Morning Chapel was always an inspiration, particularly when returning missionaries shared their experiences, trials and blessings. Games on the lawn, walks around the grounds and fellowship times together with friends all make lovely memories of Bulstrode.

A vision for the printed Word had been given to us by the Lord and we felt an enormous joy and privilege to be serving God in the WEC Press team. Sharing in the work of getting the printed Word of God out into the world was the fulfillment of that vision. David was involved in the actual printing and I was in the Press accounts. It was amazing to see the "impossible" deadlines met in answer to prayer. And when needs arose I shared in the actual "finishing" or packing of precious books and in the prayers for the safety of those books in reaching their destinations.

Life at Bulstrode meant working in the Press, duties, morning Chapel...and the children going to school in the minibus instead of walking with me. And last, but not least, learning to trust the Lord for all our needs. Pride had to go and a submissive attitude to financial provision learned and accepted. At Bulstrode we learned to trust our heavenly Father on a deeper level. Faith grew. The highs and lows of living within the Bulstrode Community enhanced our Christian lives and nurtured our character. It wasn't always easy but we learned to praise and thank the Lord in all circumstances.

When our time at Bulstrode ended in April 2000, the Lord provided all that was needed to set up Freedom Print, so we could continue printing His Word and getting it out to where it was most needed. I speak for David as well as myself when I say that living at Bulstrode was a time in our lives when the Lord richly blessed us, whilst allowing some very hard times alongside the blessings. It was a time of learning and equipping for future service. I praise Him that I can look back with thankfulness.

"Trust in the Lord with all your strength and lean not on your own understanding; in all your ways acknowledge Him and He will make straight your paths." Proverbs 3:5

Candidate Orientation

Paul Harvey

One of the main purposes of a WEC Sending Base *(or Branch)* is to select, train and prepare new members for missionary service. The Bulstrode HQ has been just one of 17 such entities around the world giving orientation to hundreds of new WECers.

In the earlier days the UK Candidate Orientation Course *(COC or CO)* lasted 4 months, but in recent times this was reduced to 10 or 12 weeks. This is still a longer period of preparation than many other Mission Agencies, but WEC maintains that a full, robust orientation process helps reduce fallout at a later stage.

Elements of the CO include the following:

*orientation to the ethos, heritage and practice of WEC

*the importance of teamwork and communication

*cross-cultural awareness, inter-generational awareness

*spiritual formation, prayer and spiritual warfare

*ministry experience and opportunities in a local church

*handling stress, health issues, practical preparation

*IT and personal security on the field

Most Candidates find CO an enjoyable and special time (Rose and I did), and many maintain a special bond with their "fellow Candidates" for the rest of their lives.

in the Candidate group photos that follow (earliest 1992, latest 2013) some faces have been obscured for security reasons as their places of service are hostile to open Christian witness *photos on this page: Richard Davey*

A Privilege

Howard Sayers

Gill and I always regarded our role as Candidate Secretaries (as we were then called) a great privilege. We had come back from Guinea-Bissau in 1981 annoyed with God for allowing ill health to mess up our service there. But after a couple of years in and out of hospital we were eventually well enough to rise to the challenge put to us to take on the Candidate Secretary role. God knew what He was doing, and as we came to accept that, we found that facilitating others to go was the next best thing to going ourselves!

During our 11 years as Candidates Secretaries we had well over 200 Candidates do the COC with us. Most of those were from the UK, but we were also blessed with a good number of other nationalities, amongst whom were wonderful people like Byungkook and Boim Yoo (who founded the WEC Sending Base in South Korea). We learnt so much from our Candidates, far more than we taught them. But it was in sharing our lives together, and our experiences of God's faithfulness, that we helped one another grow in faith and obedience.

My precious wife has been with Jesus now for over 8 years, but my guess is that she can now see, better than me, how worthwhile those 11 years were in our lives.

Practical CO

Nick Miller

Linda and I were on the 1992 Autumn Candidates' Course at Bulstrode. We thoroughly enjoyed our four months of preparation for the Spanish mission field. Everyone was expected to undertake chores of some kind and being a painter and decorator I was immediately drafted in for essential repairs and maintenance. I remember painting various bedrooms, corridors and the Main Dining Room all under the watchful eye of Norman Smith from Helps International Ministries, USA.

However, the biggest and hardest job I undertook was decorating the Main Hallway over the Main Staircase *(latterly called the Atrium)*. Our task was to paper the walls from floor to ceiling. As you can imagine this was quite a challenge. We erected a cherry picker in the centre and from there were able to reach right up to the topmost point. You may be interested to know that the longest drop of wallpaper was actually the length of one roll – 33 feet or 11m! I was in the cradle with the folded length of pasted paper smoothing it on to the wall, whilst someone gently lowered me down as and when I needed to get lower. Quite an experience and one never forgotten.

Snapshots from 12 Years at Bulstrode

Carolyn Davey

Setting off the fire alarm on our first weekend as residents: Actually, we need to blame our daughter here because she was cooking waffles with another Bulstrode kid right under the smoke detector, but even so, on our first weekend???

The joy of being Candidate Directors *(CDs)*: We say this is the best job in WEC! The reason is because Candidates are people seeking to follow Jesus wholeheartedly and the CDs have the privilege of walking alongside and getting to know them over the months that they, and we, seek God together about the way forward. During the 7 years of being Candidate Directors, over 220 candidates from 21 nationalities went to over 40 countries.

God's confirmation we should become Managers: We had been Candidate Directors for over 6 years and sensed God saying "move on", so we told the UK Directors, Stewart and Jean Moulds. Not long after, Stewart came to our office and asked if we would consider being Bulstrode Managers. To say we were surprised would be an understatement! The moment Stewart left us, we locked the office and went into the grounds, slowly walking around the Beauty Walk, talking together as thoughts tumbled out of our mouths. Half way round, we suddenly realised that we were not talking about should we take on the role of Managers, but talking of "us" in the sense of ourselves being a part of the whole team. More than that, we were even excited about the role! It was the shortest time we've ever taken when it comes to saying "yes" to something put to us.

God's timing #1: One day while we were Managers, a big chest freezer in the Kitchen failed and we needed a new one, urgently. I searched the internet for a new one but found so many possibilities I didn't know which to choose. I had to make a phone call about something else, so decided to do that instead of making a decision. When I replaced the receiver there was a voicemail message from a friend; they were moving from Gerrards Cross and the new family home wouldn't have enough room for their large chest freezer, could WEC use hers? What marvellous timing! This was just one occasion of many where God's timing was impeccable and assured me that He was in control.

God's timing #2: Bulstrode was full to the brim, every guest room was in use. A guest came up to me apologetically saying they would need to change their booking and leave that morning, a day earlier than planned and very much hoped it wouldn't be a problem. I assured them it wouldn't be. Minutes later, Moira (Accommodation Secretary) came to me saying she had a problem – she'd realised she hadn't allocated a room to someone who was arriving that day and all the rooms were booked. How lovely to be able to tell her of the conversation I'd just had and say the problem was already solved. God is good!

The Heavenly Man: The full story is told elsewhere *(p. 66)*, but the May Day when Brother Yun came must be etched in the minds of everyone who was there. Torrential rain, a traffic jam back to the M40, quite a few cars needing to be pulled out of the mud by tractor from the parking field as they left, a packed tent for the first meeting with hundreds lining up under umbrellas waiting to get a seat for the second meeting, trips to shops to get extra food because there wasn't enough in the Dining Room and people everywhere, just everywhere in the building. Yet what an incredible atmosphere of acceptance and joy – an amazing day.

Servant Leadership: At one stage while we were Candidate Directors, due to circumstances beyond our control, there was no way I was going to be able to do all the work I needed to do before the start of the next Candidate Orientation, even if I were to work 18 hours a day. I went to the UK leaders, explained the situation and asked if they could find someone from another office to help just for a few days. Sadly no one had time, but the UK Office Team knew I had painted a realistic picture, so they sent someone from their own office to help me. The ones who were the busiest, were the ones who gave of themselves – servant leadership lived out.

Autumn 2004

Beautiful Bulstrode

Rose Harvey

It was a huge step of faith as we left a comfortable 4-bedroomed house in Hemel Hempstead and a ministry and church that we loved, and made our way cautiously up the long Bulstrode drive in our small Vauxhall Astra car. Two small children were strapped into the back with all our worldly possessions around us and in a roof rack on top. It was a dark afternoon in January 1992.

The North Entrance Wing looked dark and austere as we made our approach. But what a lovely crowd of helpful WEC people greeted us! Help was instantly on hand to assist with the unpacking. This was to be the beginning of our adventure and life style with WEC.

Howard and Gill Sayers lovingly hosted 22 of us on this busy 4-month Candidate Orientation Course. As you can see from the accompanying photograph below, we were a great team and today 12 of us are still in WEC. This is testimony to God's faithfulness and our close walk with Him. These ones are truly my brothers and sisters and I love them, each one, and value their fellowship immensely.

WEC is actually not so much an organisation but a fellowship. The members are WEC. Observing the Bulstrode WEC leaders of the day really helped me to "catch on." It isn't what they said but how they *were* that I can remember. I remember Patrick Johnstone and Deiter Kuhl with their sleeves rolled up and their "pinnies" on as they obediently took their turn in the relentless Bulstrode rota system at mealtimes. This joyful attitude of service left a lasting impression on me.

below: Spring 1992 CO group photo: courtesy Chrissie Brown

Rose and husband Paul (the editor) visited Bulstrode regularly when home from Spain and were residents at Bulstrode 2007-2016

Fifteen years later, we returned to Bulstrode from WEC Spain, this time as permanent residents and Candidate Directors! It seemed a daunting position to me and sadly I struggled with what I perceived to be other peoples' expectations of me in this role. I would stress that actually it was my issue and nobody else's. Thankfully, God did release me from this bondage and actually all the Bulstrode personnel were fantastic and allowed me to be myself.

Paul and I oversaw 12 Candidate Orientation programmes, and in agreement with Carolyn Davey, I would also say that the role must be one of the best jobs there is in WEC. WEC Candidates are a very special breed of people and they come in all "shapes and sizes," whom God Himself has chosen. There is no set formula to a Candidate; whether they are single or married, with or without children, each one is precious, different, unique. These greatly cherished and to-be-esteemed workers go on to craft WEC for the future – warts an' all! Bulstrode has been a haven and a transitional home for so many in pilgrimage which of course is what we are – pilgrims this side of Heaven, greatly loved by Him who called us.

PART FOUR 2000s

Candidate Numbers

Below right are the statistics for **Candidates passing through CO in the UK** in the years **2007-2016**. Some Candidates - for example from South Korea, France and The Netherlands - come to participate in the UK CO while remaining officially linked to the Sending Base/Branch *(SB)* in their own country. Those from Finland come under the UK's oversight, as up till now there has not been a SB in Finland.

TOTAL NUMBER = 145
Average per year = 16

Source: Raine Ihalainen, Candidate Department

Hundreds more Candidates passed through in the previous 4 decades.

Spring 2012 *...with WEC artefacts, including the soundbox of CT Studd's banjo*

Candidates participating in CO at Bulstrode 2007-14 by nationality:

country	*number*	*%*
UK	74	51
South Korea	37	26
Finland	7	5
Netherlands	3	2
Nigeria	2	1.4
Kenya	2	1.4
New Zealand	2	1.4
Hong Kong	2	1.4
Germany	1	0.7
USA	1	0.7
Australia	1	0.7
Ireland	1	0.7
Cambodia	1	0.7
Malaysia/NZ	1	0.7
Belgium	1	0.7
Canada	1	0.7
Pakistan	1	0.7

Living and learning together in a multicultural CO group is tremendous fun as well as being excellent preparation for missionary service on the field. Once accepted, not only will Candidates have the challenge of adjusting to the host culture of where they are going, but they will also find themselves joining a team of WECers from many parts of the world, each having completed their own CO in their country of origin.

One particular aspect Rose and I enjoyed about the Candidate Director role was getting together with the other Candidate Directors from the different Sending Branches. It was always encouraging to compare notes and pray for one another, even though we only met up sporadically.

Mission and Me

Heather Lawrence

Twice a year, usually in spring and autumn, around 20 visitors arrive at Bulstrode for *Mission and Me*, a weekend away for spending time with God and learning more about mission.

Whilst enjoying peace in the beautiful grounds and spacious mansion, many have heard the Lord speak and challenge them. The programme is relaxed with long breaks to allow time to think, pray and chat with staff members who have experience in missions. Sessions include looking at what the Bible says about mission, from Genesis to Revelation; an overview of how God is working around the world by Operation World staff; and personal testimonies from Candidates and staff of their journey into mission. Visitors have commented on the godly atmosphere and the welcoming, friendly, relaxing environment.

photo: Anthony Lau

A highlight is usually the delicious food, especially experiencing dishes from different parts of the world as part of the Mission/ Cultural Evening. We have been blessed over many years to have WEC missionaries sharing their experiences - the surprises, joys, challenges - and giving an interactive opportunity to try learning a new language, wear local clothes, greet with a handshake/ kiss/ complicated words, sit in the correct way etc. We have gained an insight into life for a missionary in Thailand, Senegal, Brazil, Japan, Mexico, Central Asia, Chad and many more places.

The Lord has led many from *Mission and Me* to participate in short term mission trips, go to Bible College and be involved in long term mission, some with WEC.

Mission and Me has taken place at Bulstrode for over 30 years – often with 40 people a year, which amounts to over 1,000 participants. Add to that the numerous participants at other *Mission and Me* events around the country, and one can appreciate what an effective instrument *Mission and Me* has been in the Lord's hands.

below: Mission and Me group, November 2015

photo: Anthony Lau

How It Started

Francis and Mary Blackmore

As far as we remember the *Mission and Me* weekend concept was started in the 1980s, by Jean Walker in the Extension Office *(later Network Team)*. The idea was to invite young people to Bulstrode for the May Day weekend. A tailor-made programme was put on for them, leading on into the WEC Open Day on the Bank Holiday Monday. Having spent a weekend together with like-minded people and hospitable missionaries who shared their lives with them, they were more than happy to help with practical jobs while also benefiting from the special WEC meetings. Thirty-five was a good number to have; any more would have been difficult to accommodate in the mansion. When Jean Walker moved away others took on the role.

Later on, this weekend was developed and tried at different times of the year, in the spring and the autumn, and also we took a small team to start the programme in Leeds, in Scotland and in Northern Ireland. This enabled a larger number of people to travel to somewhere more local to them. There was little else like this programme at the time, and the weekends proved very popular.

photo: Anthony Lau

To be faced with questions of calling, gifting, language learning and other training, and yet at the same time to receive insights and testimonies from missionaries with cross-cultural experience, made for a very special and significant time for everyone. Of the hundreds of people we met, we are still in touch with several. Many later joined WEC or other Mission Agencies, or went into Christian ministry of some form.

Recently one friend has become an archdeacon. All of them had their eyes opened to see the needs of worldwide mission, and received a challenge to find their place in the extension of God's Kingdom. We thank the Lord for the concept of *Mission and Me*.

WEC Trek - Short Term Mission

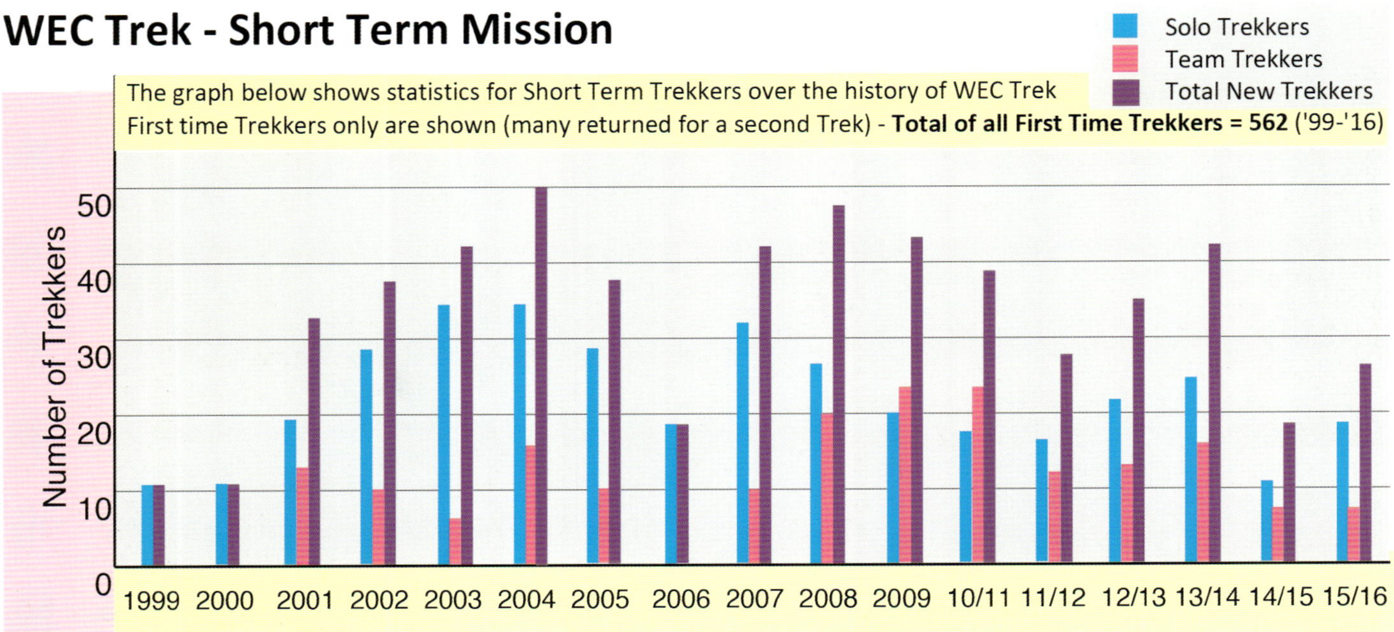

WEC Trek Beginnings

Kevin Gray

WEC Trek in the UK was started by Mary Pritchard who was based in Halesowen. She had a vision to see how a short term programme could be developed and soon the first WEC "Trekkers" were going out on individual placements to join WEC teams in different countries.

Sheila Kilkenny soon joined her and Kevin and Marja Gray also joined the WEC Trek Team in 2000. At that time Bulstrode was full and it seemed impossible for another ministry to be located there. However, there was a sense that Bulstrode would be a good location for WEC Trek especially as it could be more closely linked to the Candidate Department. WEC Youth kindly offered to share their office space with WEC Trek.

As well as individual Treks, Team Treks continued to be planned and more people joined the WEC Trek Office at Bulstrode. As space at Bulstrode became available, WEC Trek moved to their own offices (next door to the Candidates Office). The WEC Trek Office valued the fellowship at Bulstrode as did the many Trekkers who came through Bulstrode for orientation before their short-term mission trips, and for their reviews when they returned. As the graph shows, hundreds have been sent out.

My WEC Trek Trips

Eleanor Harvey

One week orientation in Bulstrode, UK. Three months in Melusi, South Africa. Three months in El Monte, Mexico. At 18, I had the chance to travel far afield, and WEC wonderfully accommodated my passion to explore continents but with an emphasis on serving Christ wherever one is.

The week orientation was alongside other solo Trekkers. I remember one lass was going off to South East Asia, while another guy was staying at Bulstrode, WEC Headquarters, to live and serve for a year. I hugely enjoyed both South African and Mexican experiences: kids' clubs, uprooting vegetable gardens, painting and decorating, horse riding, teaching English to hyper-enthusiastic children...

But what clinched it for me was serving a faithful God who has long been working across the continents and who invites us to partake and align our passions with His.

below: Eleanor in action on her WEC treks in 2010...
(left) painting a local Church building in Mexico
(right) helping with a kids' club at Melusi, South Africa - Eleanor is on the right   photos: courtesy E Harvey

photos: WEC archives Neil Rowe

Flashback: Short Term Teams USA

Short term mission has been a relatively recent development within WEC. However, before joining WEC, many WECers previously served with other Mission Agencies in a short term capacity. My wife Rose is a case in point. She spent two years on the ship, the MV Doulos, with Operation Mobilisation (OM), plus a further period at the Ship Headquarters in Mosbach, Germany. From her own experience she would confirm that a short term missionary experience can change one's life forever.

The photographs on this page take us on a flashback to the early 1980s, when short term mission teams from the USA came over several years in a row to serve God at Bulstrode. Not only do they give us a glimpse of various parts of Bulstrode being created or renovated, they also capture something of the fun, fellowship and sense of purpose that can be had when working together for the Lord.

The Day Brother Yun Came to Bulstrode

John Antill

The Heavenly Man, the remarkable story of Chinese Christian, Brother Yun, was published both in the USA and in the UK in 2002. It had an enormous impact and was voted Book of the Year 2003 by the Christian Booksellers' Convention.

Several WECers working in East Asia had either met Brother Yun or had contact with the organisation which was helping his ministry in the West. When it came to planning for May Day 2004, we felt God wanted us to see if we could arrange for him to be our main speaker. We were thrilled to hear he could come. We were conscious of the need to challenge UK churches with the needs of the mission field and to draw people from as wide a spectrum of churches as possible. The success of the book with its astonishing accounts of how God moved miraculously in Brother Yun's life meant he would attract good numbers.

We had been experiencing increasing numbers for May Day events, the highest being about 1,700 - 1,800 people and we hoped this trend would continue. So as usual we prayed earnestly for good weather and attendance for **May Day 2004** at Bulstrode.

In 2003 Brother Yun's story became increasingly well-known as the book sold fast. During the November 2003 Extension Ministries Conference someone raised a point that we should make May Day 2004 an all-ticket event. However, we were very low on administrative staff and felt we could not cope with that. We also had a history of never charging for May Day and the administration involved would have meant a charge was necessary. So we prayed and left the day to run as in previous years.

In the event the Lord sent us the most people ever to come to May Day - and the worst weather! It was estimated that 3,500 people attended in the pouring rain with queues of cars almost back to Beaconsfield trying to get in to hear Brother Yun.

Everything happened on a huge scale - the weather (pouring rain!), the huge attendance, capacity numbers in all the meetings, overwhelming response from individuals, counselling non-stop all day in the Christian Service Tent. The clearing up and cleaning operation afterwards was unprecedented too with mud tracked into the building, up the Main Stairs and on to the landing carpets - plus damage to the car-parking ground.

Lunchtime sandwiches from the Kitchen were always popular at May Day but this year there was overwhelming demand. Loudspeaker announcements were made appealing for help in the Kitchen to come and make sandwiches. The daughter of the Candidate Directors, Richard and Carolyn Davey, brought a minibus load of students to the day and there was no room for them to even eat their sandwiches at lunchtime, so they commandeered Richard and Carolyn's flat. People were overflowing from the Verandah, filling the Dining Room and Atrium to capacity, squatting on the stairs, sitting in the corridors, trying to find a place to eat out of the rain. The car park was full and beyond capacity so people had to be turned away.

Nevertheless there was a great sense of the Lord's presence that day and He was at work in people's lives. In the pre-main meeting prayer times, the platform party all stood and prayed Chinese-style* together for God to move in many hearts that day. We also prayed for a WECer who was due to testify in the main meeting but who was sick and had been ill all night. The person was healed and able to take full part. *(*praying out loud at the same time)*

All the seminars were full to capacity, as were the children's meetings in the Chapel run by Mark and Carol Callister. At the main meetings Brother Yun did not major on the sensational aspects of his testimony but he did speak in a simple, challenging way. We prayed that the Lord would greatly use his ministry in many lives. And the Lord did that, raising vision amongst that huge crowd for a lost world for Jesus. WECers were counselling people in the Christian Service Tent all day and others in the main marquee were praying for the crowds who came forward after the main meetings.

Afterwards we acknowledged a ticket system would have solved the problems. There were too many wanting to hear this man - one thing that has always saddened us is that folk who had travelled long distances could not get into Bulstrode because of the congestion. Nevertheless, we had so much for which to praise the Lord on the day the "Heavenly Man" came to Bulstrode, May Day 2004.

after the crowds and the rain

The International Office 2004-2010

Trevor and Jen Kallmier

Jen and I had the privilege of leading the IO *(International Office)* Team while based at Bulstrode from the end of 2004 through to 2010. We have many deep friendships and rich memories from our time there. Some memories that stand out...

*The Bulstrode gardens and ponds - always beautiful whether in winter or spring. As we travailed in prayer through those gardens, Jen often found herself in David's shepherd Psalm..."He restores my soul." *(Psalm 23)*

*We remember also the excitement of the Bulstrode kids as they skidded down the slopes after a good dump of snow.

*Helping to set up Bulstrode's House of Prayer for special occasions - a delight!

*Deeply earnest prayer meetings in challenging times - sensing that the whole Community of Bulstrode was at one with us as we prayed into those situations. These are special memories.

There was also the benefit of the valued input and wisdom from the UK staff; and the vital connection with OW *(Operation World)* and access to the resources of WEC UK. These were wonderful blessings for us.

I think Bulstrode has been viewed as the strategic hub for WEC for decades. Many non-UK WECers have seen Bulstrode as the "home of worldwide WEC." For us, Bulstrode was a place where many "divine appointments" occurred - unplanned by us, we had many timely meetings with folk who just happened to be passing through the base.

photo: courtesy T and J Kallmier

Trevor and Jen Kallmier, former International Directors, pictured with CT Studd's cricket bat during 2013 when WEC International celebrated its 100th Anniversary

I want to take this opportunity to honour the valuable, but often unseen, ministry of the Bulstrode staff to the numerous WECers who have stayed there. During our time we know of many who were helped, encouraged and refreshed by the care and hospitality of Bulstrode staff members. The staff went the "extra mile" in serving wider WEC. So I want to express my gratitude to the current staff and also to those who have served there faithfully in years past. Thank you!

Some years ago, the IO sensed the need to relocate to Asia. That took many years and was not an easy process for us, but we did believe God was leading us. So now WEC UK is on a similar journey, sensing God's leading for a change in its location and operation. We pray God's rich blessing on this undertaking. We will always carry very fond memories of Bulstrode and deep appreciation for the opportunity to be based there for those years. Thank you again for all those who assisted the IO team during the years spent at Bulstrode.

below: the International Office Team 2006 left to right: Young Choon, Traugott Boeker, Elaine Lee, Hanni Boeker, Anne Greaves, Trevor Kallmier, Linda Sullivan, Jen Kallmier

photo: courtesy T and J Kallmier

Our Time in the UK Leadership

John and Pauline Bagg

The *life* of a fellowship is found in the people, not the buildings. In that sense, wherever we go, the measure to which we enjoy the fullness of life that is ours in Christ will be the measure to which our fellowship and ministry thrives. That said, Bulstrode is an immense place in scope, and in impact, when you arrive up the long drive; it's a castle, a home, a mission base, a training centre, a prayer hub ... and it has been our "privilege" to live here since May 2007.

We use the inverted commas because living here has been a double-edged sword that has included both challenges and blessings. The scale of the building brings with it attendant responsibilities for adequate staffing and maintenance. Our role in leadership has been able to see this more clearly than when we were Candidates or visitors.

Our children have enjoyed living here - a great place to mix with friends, run around the fields and explore the big house. We, too, have found a number of supportive relationships, and enjoyed the various community activities that go on here throughout the year - evening football, table tennis tournaments, Bonfire Nights, Christmas, Candidates meals etc. As a family, we will look back with fondness on this season.

We have also experienced the benefit of being in both the UK Leadership Team and the wider Bulstrode fellowship - both have been sources of great encouragement and blessing. We have been in the role of UK Directors for 8 years so far, and throughout that time we've had an outstanding team. We simply couldn't do the job of "Sending Base/Ministry Centre" without them; not just because of the sheer volume of work, but more so because of the need of the variety of gifting that each one brings to the team.

Above all, we count it such a blessing that we get to work alongside like-minded people who have all signed up to being a part of seeing Christ known, loved and worshipped amongst the unreached peoples of the world. What a privilege! We trust that as we move forward into a new season for WEC International in the UK and with the relocation from Bulstrode, we will all continue to find diverse ways to express our calling, gifting and fellowship.

In recent years the walls of Bulstrode have been adorned by some of Pauline's paintings. Her inspiration often comes from themes and verses in the Bible. The painting above left recalls Isaiah's word in chapter 6:8, while the two below are based on Romans 10:13-15 and Matthew 28:19 respectively

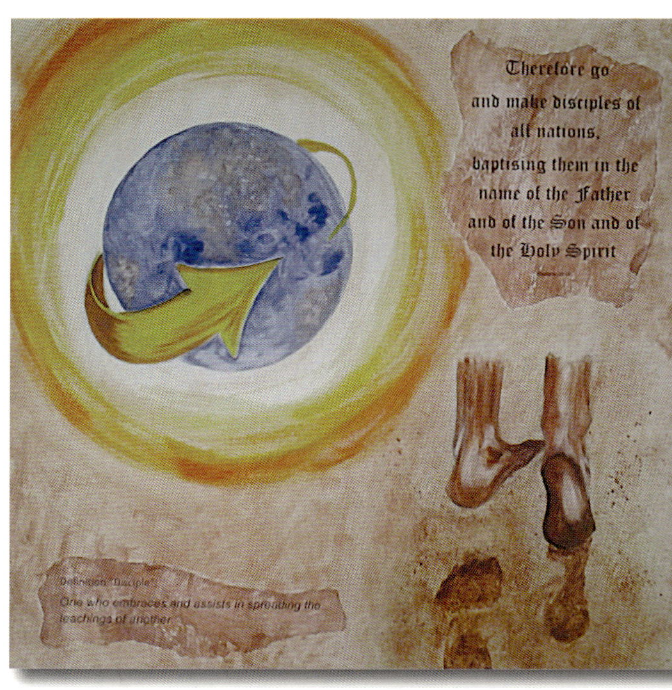

A Princess and a Spy

Dahae Jeong

My best memories of Bulstrode have been my birthday parties and "sleepovers", and I think my friends would agree that these were some of their best memories too. A lifestyle which was completely normal to me must have been so strange to them, and as a child, I took full advantage. To my friends in primary school I would pretend that I was a Korean princess and that everyone at Bulstrode were my servants. During secondary school, I no longer wanted to be a princess but a spy, so I said to my friends that Bulstrode was some sort of secret intelligence service. The Beauty Walk can be a little scary at night and I remember my friends and I filming a thriller, forcing some reluctant Volly Helpers to play the male leads.

Next to the long list of good memories there are also some not so pleasant...like repeatedly having to say goodbyes to many, many people. But the negative sides are few and I cannot thank God enough for the huge WEC family I now have, scattered all over the world. And thank God for the Boutique - my friends say I dress like an elderly person and I think it might be because the majority of my clothes are from there.

In hindsight, Bulstrode has been the most profound means of God showing me just how much He loves His children and wants to bless them. Over the years, I have experienced His unfailing, lavish provision and I have had the utmost freedom, protection and care whilst growing up. As a child, I only *felt* like a princess but years on, God has been revealing to me that I *am* one - because we are beloved sons and daughters of the King.

Happy Evenings

Judith Moulds

I moved to Bulstrode at the age of 13 after spending my childhood overseas. Moving to the UK was a big adjustment, but living at Bulstrode was a huge blessing in this time of transition. Having other MKs *(Missionary Kids)* and Voluntary Helpers around gave me an immediate community.

I have happy memories of evenings spent playing football, volleyball and table tennis, of bonfires, "sardines" and dressing up in clothes from the Boutique. To be honest, most of what we did was not exciting - walking to the BP garage to buy an ice cream, or sitting in Reception asking the question, "What shall we do?" - but it was good to be together.

I remember the horror I felt when I set off the fire alarm by cooking waffles under a smoke detector - obviously an accident. I remember a group of MKs volunteering to renovate a room, wanting to use our limited finances to bless someone coming to Bulstrode. We really had no idea what we were doing, but were supported by the Managers who saw our hearts despite our complete lack of skills. We discovered then that painting the outside window frames of a listed building bright blue is not a good idea, and that it takes a lot longer to cover over afterwards than to paint in the first place!

I'm really thankful to God that I got to spend so much time at Bulstrode. It's always hard to know where "home" is as an MK, but this was definitely one of mine.

below: "Princess Dahae" views the grounds *photo: Hwa Jeong*

We lived above the front door, and one Sunday morning my son leaned out of the window, dressed as Robin Hood with his bow and arrow and shouted, "Stop, no one can come in!" Colin Nicholas was just about to come in through the front door after church, but he looked up and then engaged in a 'battle' for Bulstrode.

Refuge from the Storms

Naomi Ettrick

Bulstrode has always been a huge part of my life. One of the greatest experiences of my life was living abroad, as an MK *(Missionary Kid)*; and the hardest has been returning. Bulstrode has really helped me with that. It has always been a place for renewal and refreshment, a place for reading and exploring, eating and playing football in the evenings. I don't regret a single moment spent there, because it really was a representation of God on earth. The atmosphere of love and service, God's people all in one place combined with the beauty of the grounds and the security of the mansion itself has made Bulstrode a refuge from the storms in life, a place where God seems close, and real to me.

The first thing my sister and I would do upon arrival was to try and "get lost" and search through the building for the *Love, Joy, Peace* tapestries. I remember crossing multiple fields in search of the horses, spending ages trying to get close to them, and many more hours reading in the Library or hiding in the woods.

I can't believe I will have to lose it now. It has always been so constant and stable. I know that losing it will be as hard as leaving "the mission field" for everyone, not only me. I pray for us all, that we can find God's likeness in other ways, in each other and across the world as we search for that same place of sanctuary that Bulstrode has always been, to me.

The Swirly Branches

Daniel Honman

I have many special memories from Bulstrode, the place where we lived when I was born. Actually I lived there most of my life. We left when I was nine and now I am ten years old. One of my memories is the den. It was just over the stone bridge where there are lots of swirly branches .We liked that place because it had good trees to climb and has beautiful trees all tangled together.

Our son was always wandering off, he was only two. So we put clogs on his feet so you always knew where he was by the tap tap tapping of his feet.

Best and Worst

Caitlin Bagg

My best memory of Bulstrode would have to be all the bonfires that we have had, especially when all my friends were still here. One Bonfire Night I burnt my hand on a sparkler and had to put cling film all over my hand. Also when Natalie was still here with me we got up to all sorts of mischief like climbing things we shouldn't be climbing.

To add to my bonfire memory of Bulstrode...my actual favourite Bonfire Night was when me, Natalie, Lydia and Hannah all sang Karma Chameleon to everyone and I was the only one who actually knew the song - so I was basically singing it on my own!

The naughtiest thing...In roughly about 2010 when I was about 7 or 8, I was given a brand new luminous pink pen. While I was in the mansion I decided to draw a long line on the wall from Reception all the way to some of the upstairs toilets. My mum followed the line and found me at the end of it and I was made to clean the walls myself the next day. I even got my pink pen taken off me!

photo: Sam Harvey

Dens and 'Smores

Lydia Honman

I have lived in Bulstrode practically all my life because I moved there with my mum and dad when I was nine weeks old. My favourite memory was playing in the dens we found, then when the season changed we found new ones. While we were doing that we explored new parts of Bulstrode that we had never encountered before. Another memory was playing hide and seek in the Bulstrode grounds; that was really fun as we normally hid in the bushes not minding the fact that we would be found really easily and that the leaves scratched us.

I remember playing in Bulstrode when it was snowing and sledging down the hills. I also remember watching the fireworks every Bonfire Night and toasting marshmallows by the "kids' bonfire" (a mini-fire instead of the massive bonfire) so kids can get close to it and have 'smores'*. I will really miss Bulstrode because all my childhood memories are centered there. It will be hard to let them go. *(*toasted marshmallow/chocolate snacks)*

Childhood Highlights

Sheena Wardrope

1969 - My 11th birthday party in the Keep. It was a cold late November day but we had a roaring fire in the enormous fireplace in which we baked potatoes and melted marshmallows.

Sometime in the 1970s - Meeting Cliff Richard when he came with his church for a weekend conference.

The Christmas Show - Every Christmas, during my teenage years at least, the staff and MKs at Bulstrode put on an evangelistic Christmas drama/concert and buffet for the people in the local area that we came into contact with. The people from the post office, school teachers, hairdressers, GPs etc. My Maths teacher did not believe in God but he and his wife came every year and he said he always looked forward to it.

The naughtiest things - well one of them! - In the early 1970s, when I was in my early teens, Bulstrode was very busy and often full to capacity. It was understood by resident staff that if they were away for some reason, visitors might have the use of their room if the guest rooms were all full. A notice of all guests and the rooms to which they were allocated was kept on the main notice board.

Another WEC MK and I decided to play a trick on a member of staff on the day she returned from duties away from Bulstrode. We "invented" a guest, put the fictitious person's name, dates of her stay and the room number on the board, making it clear that she would have left the day before the WEC staff member's return. We then went into the bedroom, closed the curtains, stuffed the bed with pillows, put a slightly deflated football on the pillow, covered it with a wig and generally left the room looking like someone was fast asleep in the bed. The trick worked in that the person whose room it was got a terrible shock when she opened the door and thought she had disturbed a guest who had stayed longer than expected. We got found out though... and if the staff member referred to is reading this, I hope we are forgiven!

And lastly, I can also tell you that my brother, Martin Rowe, and another MK hid every single toilet roll in the building before dawn one April Fools' Day.

Lily Pond - the boat is no longer there!

When our son was about three, he was very close friends with another MK, a little girl of the same age. They decided they were going to get married, so they went to the Management Office and asked if they could please get married at Bulstrode.

Freedom to Wander

Miriam Harvey and Serene Ellis

Miriam came to Bulstrode in 2007 aged 7 and Serene came in 2010 aged 9. Here they tell their story:

Bulstrode's a great place for playing games – hide and seek, water fights, playing on the swings. It's huge and we have freedom to wander around the place. It's also safe for us to have sleepovers in the Courtyard Lounge. There are movie nights and Teen Camp reunions when we meet up with friends from Camp. We've been into just about every room there is, including the Tower where we once found a dead shrew. Another time we caught two newts in the Lily Pond.

When visiting groups come we often help Moira (in charge of accommodation) by showing people to their rooms. At Easter when the Chapel was turned into a 24/7 Prayer Room we took the 3am-5am slot and produced paintings and nailed prayer requests on to the wooden cross.

Our biggest disaster was when we made a big hole in the corridor wall. One of us (Miriam) was pushing the other (Serene) in the wheelchair, which sits by the front door, for fun. We heard someone coming so went faster, and Serene's foot went through the wall. We couldn't hide it so we had to confess. Mike (in charge of maintenance) made sure we helped fix it, by teaching us to saw the wood, drill holes, sandpaper and paint the wall like new.

Capsized!

John and Margaret Mills

One May Day event when our son Andrew was about 12, he and a friend were exploring the grounds while we were in the marquee at one of the meetings. The boys came to the Lily Pond and saw an old rowing boat upturned beside it. So they decided to have some fun. Out in the middle of the lake they realised there was a hole in the bottom of the boat and soon they capsized and were in the water. I was called out of the meeting and found Andrew had had a hot bath (I believe provided by Jill Sayers) and clothes from the Boutique to go home in!

When the Nursery was running, one of the girls took all the others into the toilet and solemnly got them all to wash their face – in the water from the toilet bowl.

Magical Place

Freda van Norel (née Cook)

My name is Freda van Norel. I was born in 1968 as Freda Cook in Chad, Africa. My parents are WEC missionaries. This meant that Bulstrode was very much part of my life as a kid, especially in the 1970s and 80s. We were always taken along to meetings and seminars whenever we were in England, and sometimes spent up to a few weeks there. I remember the excitement when the car would turn into the driveway and we knew we would see the house round the next bend. "Uncle Neil's Castle" we called it, and for many years I was under the impression that this wonderful place belonged solely to Neil and Mary Rowe, whom I loved more than my own aunts and uncles.

My favourite memory? Where do I start? I was always a dreamer, and relived so many fairy tales and stories at Bulstrode. I loved the gardens, where I had all my secret places. The big tree by the pond that you could climb, and if you lay flat on one of the big branches, no one could see you from below. Did you know that that Lily Pond was a place where many romances flourished? And if yours was one, that there was a little girl up in the tree who might have witnessed it? But don't worry, I never told anyone.

I was a nature-lover, and spent many very happy hours just observing in the gardens and woods, collecting all sorts of insects and letting them go afterwards. I also loved the house, and would secretly climb up into the Tower and pretend that that little room was mine. I was never sure whether I was actually allowed up there and I never asked, in case the answer was "no."

And of course, the folly (Keep) in the garden where we played table tennis; and I played at being held captive and being rescued by a prince on a white horse. The WEC Teen Camp reunions where we would crawl into each other's bedrooms and spend all night screeching with laughter, building up friendships, keeping the whole house awake, and crawling along the secret passageways to escape being caught by the leaders.

One day I got lost in the passageways with my cousin. We must have been gone for a long time. We heard our names being called over the intercom, time and time again, and I remember thinking how silly it was for them to ask us to "please come to the Reception" when there was no way we could find it! This was obviously the time my parents thought I was very naughty, even though I really didn't mean to be. When we finally opened a door and found ourselves in the Main Hall, very near to the front door, we were confronted by pretty frantic parents. I wondered what the fuss was about; it wasn't as if we had left the house, and I wished for Narnia, where you could be gone for ages without anybody missing you.

For me, Bulstrode was definitely always that magical, mystical place, and I am so thankful to have been allowed to be a part of it.

magical carpet of pink

Palm Tree that survived!

Target Practice

Jeanne Buchanan

My son John was at boarding school in the UK while I was in Colombia, and there he made a cross-bow in class. He had visited Bulstrode a few times and made friends with some of the other teenagers there, so one weekend he took his cross bow. He says: "I remember killing a fat pigeon that belonged to a retired missionary. We prayed for the pigeon the next morning."

Fire from Heaven

John Tromans

We once went away for a few days leaving our boys at Bulstrode in the care of my parents. It was during the Retired Workers Conference and Dan, Phil and Nathan decided this would be a good time to set one of the palm trees on fire - the ones on the Lime Avenue which were in full view of the main lounge! "Let the fire from heaven fall!"

Best Swings Ever

Ulrike Hunt (née Kuhl)

My parents are Dieter and Renate Kuhl, who were WEC's International Secretaries from 1985 to 1998. I was at Bulstrode in the 1980s and have so many memories....

1. Playing wide games in the grounds. There was a bunch of us around the same age. In the summer months, when the days were long, we would play "capture the flag" type games - wonderful, as there were so many places to hide in the bushes. We still had access to the Long Water then. I remember one summer Peter Johnstone had a canoe on the lake that we all had a go in.

2. The swings were the best ever - so high!

3. Hiding away in our flats on May Day and hating being inundated by people visiting.

4. Meeting up with the other teenagers at supper time and chatting.

5. Sometimes we were allowed a party in the Keep. One time we had music, dancing, games, and food up there. We were joined by our friends from the Gold Hill Church Youth Group.(1987?)

6. We used to play in the "cave" - the underground vaults accessed from the bank. Once Tim Johnstone and Tim Sayers, convinced that there was a secret passage from there to the Bull Hotel, crawled through a tight tunnel, coming out at the bottom of the garden. I went down a few yards but chickened out.

7. Borrowing the Boutique key and having a good laugh at all the clothes down there.

8. Once in a while we were allowed to sleep in a guest room. I remember one particular sleepover in about 1985, which included a midnight feast and lots of giggling.

9. It was fun having weekend lunch with friends in the Dining Room. It was usually sausages and beans on a Saturday and roast chicken thighs on a Sunday.

10. The red minibus that would take us to Gerrards Cross to catch the school bus and being picked up again at the end of the day.

11. A moonlit walk in the gardens with my fiancé after a youth group barbecue.

12. Having our wedding reception at Bulstrode...

13. In the winter of '85 the Lily Pond froze over. A Dutch WECer had his skates and skated on the pond. We followed suit - though we didn't have skates. That was the only year we ever got to walk on the island in the middle of the Lily Pond. That winter we also had fun sledging in the fields outside.

14. Once, walking back from Gerrards Cross on my own I realised the cows were running full pelt downhill towards me. I was convinced my time had come, but thankfully they parted and ran past me. That was my scariest moment.

There were definitely fun things about being a teenager in Bulstrode - there were others my age and we got on well. The downside was that whenever you cycled anywhere it was always uphill. It was also a bit remote in that we always needed a lift to get out (or cycle uphill!). I did at times wish I was living in a normal house in a normal street. Kids at school thought we lived in some sort of commune.

the Lily Pond also froze over in the winter of 2009 below: the editor's family - Eleanor skating, the others on the island

Home in my Memory

Rachel McNulty (née Parker)

While Bulstrode might just be a building, it holds many memories and is a place where great faith and the values of WEC have been lived out over the years. As a resident you see and experience countless stories of God's faithfulness and provision in the lives of many others who have lived there or passed through. Since 1998 I've lived at Bulstrode for seven years in total, having grown up there as a teenager, returned after university and then again later as an adult to do CO and work for a while (if you had tried to tell the teenage me that would happen, I would have laughed at you). Throughout that time there were also various visits back to see friends and family. From my persepctive as an MK, other homes may come and go but Bulstrode has been the one that has remained. Many things might change but Bulstrode (despite staff turnover) always felt the same - coming up the drive always felt like coming home.

For many MKs our home is a place that only exists in our memories, as it's made up of times and people that no longer exist in the same place. For me Bulstrode (and in a different way Changi Airport) has always been my familiar home. Many MKs have had their weddings or wedding photos at Bulstrode, me included, because it holds a sense of belonging and home for us. I mean...where else do you get an instant community of MK friends who "get" you and whose parents push them out the door to go and make the new kids feel welcome?

Living at Bulstrode was not always easy - it had its own set of unique frustrations at every stage of life - but it has given me a place to meet some of my best friends and has instilled in me many WEC values through the lives of WECers I've met there. To me it was so normal to be serving in the Bulstrode Kitchen or preparing for May Day/GOFest alongside someone in international leadership, that I almost forgot that for most organisations this would be totally unheard of. Now that I'm in WEC (by my own choice this time) I really value the fact that, thanks to Bulstrode, I know so many people living and working throughout the world.

Bulstrode holds many memories...

*playing sardines in the Basement, hidden behind a suitcase on a shelf unseen by the Manager, only to make a quick escape once he moved on (hardly safe, but seriously, as a teenager, how could you *not* play sardines in such an awesome space?!)

*way too many memorable Voluntary Helpers to mention

*hours spent in the Reception area chatting and wondering what to do before deciding it's too late to do anything so going to bed

*such fun with our crazy Candidate group

*summer and Christmas holidays

*volleyball games

*great fashion choices from the Boutique

*and great times seeing the place abuzz with a missions focus for May Day/GOFest with everyone running around, stressed out, while the Manager, Norman (Cuthbert), sits quietly in Reception reading the paper, saying it will all work itself out.

And I love how you can tell the era that someone lived at Bulstrode by how they refer to various flats; is it the Carruthers', Rounds' or Ellis's flat, or the Glovers', Grays' or Lawrences'? It has been a real privilege to get to know so many people through Bulstrode and as an MK it will continue to be home in my memory, even as the function of the building changes. All I learnt there and the friendships made will last, and I pray that the sense of community and support will continue in new ways.

dramatic lighting in the Bulstrode gardens

We Met at Bulstrode

Peter and Tanja's Story

Tanja and I met as Candidates on the Spring 2010 Candidate Orientation *(CO)* at Bulstrode. As we began to get to know each other, we realised that we both sensed God calling us to serve Him among the same people group in the same (small) area of the Middle East - and even that He was leading us to do this together, as a married couple. We also sensed some urgency in this and were married within five months of the CO finishing.

Life has been quite a whirlwind over the past five years since then, taking us on a surprising, and often challenging journey through Finland (Tanja's home)...the UK...and the deserts of the Middle East - and we've been blessed with a beautiful little boy along the way.

This strange journey, with all its challenges, has often stretched us far beyond our own resources or ability to cope, but we can testify to the great faithfulness of our Father God and give thanks for the special memories we have of starting this great journey of love together in the beauty of Bulstrode in early spring.

Donald and Rosangela's Story *(pictured above)*

Donald: I came down to Bulstrode from the West Coast of Scotland in May 2008. This was to work as a volunteer for three months, after I had had to give up my job. I knew that the Lord was leading me to missionary service, but I wasn't sure in what field or what organisation. So I came down to Bulstrode to check out WEC, see how they operated, and to "spy out the land."

I didn't know what I was going to do after this time, so I committed the three months to praying and seeking what the Lord had for me next. And I didn't have to wait long. During my first week I met a beautiful Brazillian woman called Rosangela. I introduced myself to her on our first meeting and tried to start some conversation, but she didn't seem very interested. She was on her way from Brazil to Senegal, and had stopped some months at Bulstrode to improve her English. She was very focused on her mission and did not want any distractions!

However, as the days passed we gradually got to know each other better and enjoyed one another's company. Around this time another Brazillian WECer passed through Bulstrode on her way to Chad, and noticed something between us. She ended up being our matchmaker. This was fine for a shy Scotsman who didn't know what to do anyway!

God spoke to us both individually and clearly. We had only known each other a couple of weeks, but we had God's peace that it was indeed His leading and will. So Bulstrode is a ***very*** special place for us, holding many good memories.

Has God a Sense of humour? **Rosangela:** It was June 2008 when I found myself at Bulstrode to improve my English and then to go to Senegal. But with more understanding of the language came mixed feelings and uncertainty about my future.

I had just been in touch with the Senegal Field Leader, Keith Gibson, and we realised that a misunderstanding had occurred. I was trained for both language analysis and Bible translation. I was going for one and they were expecting me for the other. Keith wisely said, "I need to be honest with you, we don't have any work for analysis of language and I can't see any starting up in the next two years. Let's stop here and pray again for God's leading for your future."

In that same month as we prayed for God's leading, a man from Scotland arrived...his name: Donald Fraser. I have to confess that it wasn't love at first sight as I was determined to keep my eyes focused on the future ministry for me, and also I confess my judgment was just by appearance. I misjudged Donald as just a lump of muscle and not much else; and another thing, he would be always dirty as he was working in the Bulstrode grounds...not a very attractive sight to me.

Through a Brazilian friend, Miriam, I had the opportunity to be with Donald a few times, listening when he shared more about himself, and of course being cleaner. I could see he was a very special man, searching for God's will for his life.

I told my mentor, Margie Whitehorn about this man who had shared his feelings, and Margie, as special as she is, said to me: "I don't know what you should do, but let's pray." As I was leaving the room, suddenly she said that she had a word from God: ***" 'For I know the plans I have for you,'*** **declares the Lord,** ***'plans to prosper you and not to harm you, plans to give you hope and a future'."*** That was a beautiful experience; for the first time I had been so blessed in English. I said thanks and left the room making a simple prayer: "God would you speak with Donald please? I will not, I don't want him with my conviction, he needs his own."

That week, as we both shared our weaknesses, hopes and fears for the future, Donald shared about his health and also said to me, "I know nothing but deerstalking; have you ever seen a deerstalker on the mission field? What can I do for the Kingdom of God?" We then read his Daily Bread devotional, which he hadn't yet read that day. When he started, it was beautiful: ***" 'For I know the plans I have for you,'*** **declares the Lord,** ***'plans to prosper you and not to harm you, plans to give you hope and a future'."*** *(Jeremiah 29:11)* I knew then God was there and it was Him talking to us and in that particular moment to Donald. Donald continued the devotional: "Don't you know what you can do? Put into My hands who you are, and I will show you what I can do with you. I will give you a future and hope. I will bless you!"

God has indeed fulfilled His Word. Over seven years we have seen his love, guidance, provision and encouragement, as he uses us for His purposes. **Has God a sense of humour?** The way God led us; bringing Donald from the cold, rainy Highlands and me from the heat of Brazil and all the differences that brings; well, I think you have the answer!

rare Roble Beech, native species to Chile

boathouse with Weeping Willow and Horse Chestnut Tree

majestic Magnolia

towering Tulip Tree

Andy the Handyman - for such a Time as this

Paul Harvey

God's remarkable provision over five decades for running and maintaining Bulstrode has come not only in financial terms. Often He has also provided just the right skilled personnel at just the right time.

Andy Pool arrived to help at Bulstrode on 29th June, 2009 - one of the UK's hottest days on record. His first job was fixing the windows of the Children's Nursery, and he remembers the blast of heat escaping as he removed the windows from the greenhouse-like room. He had come to offer his practical skills on a temporary basis - seven years later he is still fixing, repairing, improving, and even restoring Bulstrode to its former glory. Here is an overview of his seven years' voluntary work at Bulstrode.

Andy had been a construction site manager, but with the economic downturn of the previous year there was now no building site to manage. Knowing a little about WEC, mainly through his sister who was a member at Gold Hill Baptist Church, Andy made contact with Bulstrode. The Manager at the time, Richard Davey, was naturally interested in someone willing to help with the never-ending task of maintaining Bulstrode.

In the early months, Andy worked alongside staff member Brian Beakhouse, who was soon giving him increased responsibilities, realising that here was a professional craftsman who could turn his hand to almost anything. As the refurbishment of the large rooms in the Main House kicked in, Andy found himself involved in major repair work – tearing rooms apart, patching up stairs, brick-laying, re-plastering and carpentry. The huge Victorian rooms with high ceilings had been converted years earlier into partitioned accommodation space - the task now was to renovate them to their original dimensions and grandeur. Andy was the man for the job.

In the Turret Room (a circular-shaped annexe to the Verandah Lounge), the false ceiling was removed, revealing not only two lovely stained glass windows that had been out of sight for decades, but also the fact that the tall wooden shutters had been sawn in two to facilitate the false ceiling. "Butchery" Andy called it, before restoring it for use. The winding staircase between the Verandah Lounge and Balcony Lounge, which had been closed off for decades, also revealed its secrets. First, the original long, curving banister was discovered lying dormant, but salvageable - Andy duly salvaged and re-hung it. Second, he and Brian discovered a piece of Victorian ingenuity for bringing light down from the roof to the dark, understairs nook of the house. The removal of paint from a circular disc in the ceiling, revealed that it was actually transparent glass, and that there was a vertical shaft, which formerly would have allowed natural light to travel all the way down from the roof through the house.

Andy's expertise and experience proved useful in other areas of the house. In order to comply with health and safety regulations, a second fire escape route was needed for the new rooms in the attic to be habitable. Andy organised the construction of a new link passageway between the two pitched roofs of the main building. There was also considerable debate about the new Library, specifically how to accommodate several tons of books in such a large, open room situated on the first floor above the Dining Room. Andy had noticed masses of seashells under the floorboards – apparently a Victorian method of noise insulation – so he suggested removing the weight of these. In all, seven tons of shells were sent down the chute into the skip below! *(p. 89)*

For almost seven years, five days a week, Andy has been the first in through the Bulstrode gates, having travelled the thirty-odd miles from his home in Chessington. I asked him why he kept on coming over so many years. The reasons he gave were:

*He enjoys turning up the driveway on a frosty morning and seeing the horses in the meadow with icicles hanging from their eyelids, while pheasants scuttle across the road.

*He relishes the glorious fragrance of the large Silver Lime in July, which pervades the garden and car park.

*And he loves meeting the missionaries who pass through, the uplifting prayer times and the family atmosphere of Bulstrode.

below left: stained glass window in the turret part of the Verandah Lounge revealed after decades of being hidden

below: the large Silver Lime tree (more photos re. Andy p. 89)

Volly Helpers (also known as Vollies)

Alex (Spain) and Rahel (Germany)

I, Rahel, arrived at Bulstrode early in 2013. After six months as a Volly I had the opportunity to serve as the Catering Manager. In my experience as a Volly, I could enjoy the fellowship with the other Vollies. Even though we grew up in different cultures, we share the same faith and the same love for God. In my time as Catering Manager, I could learn to serve the Lord in all areas and at all times. It doesn't matter what we are doing or where, to serve Him should be our main priority. I am also thankful to God because in my time in Bulstrode I was able to meet my future husband. I am so pleased to God for bringing me the chance to spend one year and a half in Bulstrode, because through that I could grow more in Him and He presented me with brothers and sisters forever.

I, Alex, came to Bulstrode in the last months of 2013, October to be more accurate. I served as a Volly for nine months. I had the chance to share so many experiences with people from different backgrounds. It was great to learn how to understand each other and share similar perspectives of God. During this course in Bulstrode I could stop, reflect and listen to what God had prepared for my life. In our daily lives we are full of tasks and we ask so many things of our Father but we rarely stop to listen for what He wants for our lives. It was such a great experience to talk with different missionaries and to learn from people who had lived in extreme situations and hear what they had learnt from them about God. During my time here, God brought me the woman after God's heart who will become my wife soon, if God wills. I praise the Lord for bringing me to this marvellous place.

Alex Trinidad and Rahel Grossmann *(below)*

Martin (back row, centre) with Volly group, November 2015

Martin (Czech Republic)

For me, Bulstrode means adventure. There is an opportunity to meet someone new or find out something new every day. Bulstrode is changing but God seems to be in that change. So, for me, most importantly, Bulstrode means hearing God and obeying what He has said. Bulstrode means prayer and life to the full.

Martin Korábečný *- also pictured opposite, serving, 3rd from left*

Hundreds of young people like these, from many countries, have spent time at Bulstrode serving as volunteers or "Volly Helpers." Many have gone on to full-time Christian work.

Jessica (Brazil) *above: Jessica (centre) with fellow Vollies*

On my last day at Bulstrode, a very dear friend gave me a little gift. It was a key holder with a sweet elephant on it. Then she told me: "Jessica, we have a saying in English that goes: 'Elephants never forget.' This is to remind you that we'll never forget about you and you will never forget about us."

Over two years later I must confess - she was right! Whoever I am with, I always share something that I've learned during my time in Bulstrode. From how to make jacket potatoes to how to pray for the nations. I've learned to serve God and others with my best in everything I do. I would say that in Bulstrode I had a small glimpse of how it will be like when the Kingdom comes. I could honestly say that part of who I am today, and a very good part, is due to the blessed and unforgettable time that God gave me in Bulstrode!

Jessica Mesquita, Volly Helper from July 2013 to December 2013.

Kitchen Volunteers

Chris and Kay Witty

photo: courtesy C and K Witty

Walking into Reception at Bulstrode has always felt like coming home for us. From the first time, over nine years ago, there was something that gripped our hearts. We have never worked out what it is but there is a distinctive smell that warms the Entrance Hall. It is ingrained and ever-constant, never changing over the years. When we get to Reception and take a deep breath we are immediately blessed.

We first came to Bulstrode for a *Mission and Me* weekend *(see p. 63)* in November 2006; that weekend changed our lives. We had travelled up from Cornwall, accompanied by a friend and I can remember being overwhelmed by the building and the prospect of being surrounded by so many holy people! Needless to say, in true Bulstrode fashion, everyone was kind, caring and interested in our lives, making us feel so comfortable and at ease. We returned to Cornwall knowing that somehow Bulstrode would play a part in our lives.

After a WEC trek *(see p. 64)* together as a couple and voluntary redundancy, I (Kay) found myself travelling to Bulstrode again to volunteer for a couple of weeks (or so I thought) before returning home to look for work. I was placed in the Kitchen, cracking thirty eggs at a time instead of the three I was used to. The constant traffic through the kitchen was a real blessing, listening to tales of life as a WEC missionary from people from all over the globe; what a unique place and what a privilege to have met so many wonderful people with so many amazing stories.

The weeks passed...returning to Cornwall just didn't happen. Before long the Lord had moved us from Cornwall to enable us to be more involved at Bulstrode. The Kitchen has remained our home whenever we can and we have enjoyed the challenge of cooking exotic dishes from around the globe for various *Mission and Me* weekends.

In 2017 we finally go overseas ourselves. It has taken some time but the Lord has used Bulstode in a way that nothing else could do. It has been there, filled with so many wonderful people who are ready to give, pray, encourage, advise, challenge and share their lives. The constant love and acceptance that we've experienced within the walls of Bulstrode has blessed us beyond measure. We are very privileged to have been even a small part of it. There is a season for all things under heaven; our season sharing life at Bulstrode has changed our lives and blessed us with so many dear friends, and we will never forget it.

photo: Anthony Lau

English at Bulstrode

In return for the work they put in, Volly Helpers at Bulstrode receive free board and lodging as well as classes in English. Over the years, many volunteer teachers have given time to the task of teaching English to them. ***Derryck Orridge****, until recently the Coordinator of the English Teaching programme, describes this aspect of Bulstrode life:*

For months the clock over the English Language Classroom stood still at twenty-five to eleven. That's just after the morning coffee break has begun. A helpful symbol, reminding us where and when the real language-learning takes place. One afternoon a week in the classroom helps - but it's only a small part of the language-learning process.

As teachers, we always like to think that learning revolves around us, and this feeling is only enhanced by the Voluntary Helpers' obvious enthusiasm for English classes. It takes a while before the realisation sets in that an afternoon in class is a welcome relief from the hard work around the building that is the usual lot of the Voluntary Helpers.

One of the reasons that young people give for wanting to come to Bulstrode is "to improve my English." To spend time with God, and to grow spiritually, are other reasons given. Washing sheets or weeding the garden are rarely given as motivating factors, although all tasks are tackled with enthusiasm once the Volly Helpers are here.

Those same attitudes of willingness and co-operation are carried over into English classes. That's why it's such a pleasure to teach at Bulstrode. There's huge satisfaction in seeing and hearing the progress made by students after a few months here - that might be because of, or despite the teaching, but in the end it doesn't really seem to matter!

25 to eleven - time for coffee break!

Variety the Spice of Life

Sometimes Bulstrode residents have ended up taking on a variety of different roles. ***Gillian Armstrong*** *describes her unique mix:*

I came to Bulstrode in September 2004 and have done a variety of things. In fact some things have come full circle. I started off working in the Kitchen, Bulstrode Bookroom and Children's Resources. Then I spent most of my time in the Management Team but for physical reasons I had to step down from there. I have worked in the Library, Household and Reception. After leaving the Management Team I started working in WEC Publications. At the time of writing I still work in the Kitchen, and have started to work in the Bookroom again. I am also looking after the resources in the Youth Office.

Outside of my work for Bulstrode I have been teaching various musical instruments, mainly to the children of staff, but for a year I also had outside pupils. During this time I have taught a range of instruments and have taken one person up to Grade 6 piano. The instruments taught include piano, clarinet, violin, flute, saxophone and recorder.

I have enjoyed Chapel times and meal times and learning new skills. My favourite times and most challenging times have been working with our Voluntary Helpers. Favourite, because I like to teach them how to make the meals I cook and like learning from them. Challenging because of difficulty in understanding each other especially when they first arrive. God has definitely mellowed me during my time here and has increased my patience.

As well as my involvement at Bulstrode I have been involved with things outside. I have sung in various choirs, been involved with children's work at church, playing in the bands and playing the piano for communion at some of the local Residential Homes.

Gillian (right) teaching Miriam piano

1

Missionary Highway - Resurfacing the Bulstrode Drive

Anthony Franks

In the days of horse and carriage, three tracks descended the hill on which Bulstrode Manor stood - to London, to Windsor and to Bath (the first two can still be traced across the horse field). In the 1940s the Royal Air Force laid a new concrete road between the Bulstrode entrance and the A40, the Oxford Road. In WEC's 49 years, many thousands of visitors and residents (as well as our neighbours) have utilised this driveway. Anthony takes up the story of the resurfacing of this "missionary highway":

Many will recall the negotiating skills required to avoid the pothole hazards of the Bulstrode drive! The culprits, of course, were the concrete slabs which the road was made of in eons gone by. Many years after the road was first constructed, tarmac was laid on top of the slabs but, with the passing of time, cracking within and movement between the slabs resulted in a gradually increasing network of potholes and crevasses in the tarmac.

In 2011 it was decided to remove the old tarmac, fill in the cracks with a flexible material and then overlay with new tarmac - the intention being to try and minimise the recurrence of the cracking problem.

The photographs show the following sequence of events:

1 The drive as it was prior to the work being carried out *(opposite page below)*

2 a & b The cattle grid and removal

3 a & b The old tarmac being removed from the top of the concrete slabs and a typical crack in a concrete slab

4 a & b The resurfacing work in progress and the finished article!

photos: Anthony Franks

Bulstrode and the Body of Christ

Paul Harvey (information kindly provided by Moira Stephen)

Bulstrode has been a great venue for a huge range of groups to come and meet with God, conduct their business, or simply enjoy fellowhsip and fun in the grounds. WEC has rejoiced in making the facilities available to the whole Body of Christ. Below are just some of the groups who have enjoyed Bulstrode in recent years. Apologies if your group is missing.

Churches and Church groups

Beaconsfield URC
Berkhamsted Baptist Church
Chenies Baptist Church
Cherith Chapel, High Wycombe
Chinese Church in London
Crown Church, Hillingdon
Croxley Green Baptist Church
Farnham & Hedgerley Community Church
Gold Hill Baptist Church
Hillingdon Park Baptist Church
Hillingdon Pentecostal Church
Hope Church, Beaconsfield
Hounslow Evangelical Church
International Presbyterian Church
Korean Ealing Church
Little Kimble Baptist Church
London Korean Church
Majesty Christian Centre
New Church, Hemel Hemsptead
Oxford Korean Church
Ruislip Baptist Church
Rayners Lane Baptist Church
Rayners Lane Youth Group
Raynes Park Korean Church
St Aldates Church, Oxford
St James Church, Gerrards Cross
Seer Green Baptist Church
Tyndale Baptist Church, Reading
Waterloo Road Church, Uxbridge
Wycliffe Baptist Eldership, Reading

Mission Agencies and Organizations

Betel Groups
Christian Camps International
Christian Literature Crusade
Church of God Evangelism
Cross Teach Trust
David Garrison Hope for Muslims Tour
Deo Gloria Trust
EQUIP
Frontiers Orientation Groups
Gideons International
GOFest Event and Planning Meetings
International Mobilisation Mission
Keep in Touch
Kairos Council and Groups
Kollide-a-scope Puppets
Korean Missionary Council Meeting
London Korean Mission Conference
Roving Artists
Sharpening Your Interpersonal Skills
St Peters Children - Fun in a Field
UCCF Central Forum (University and Colleges Christian Fellowship)
World Harvest Mission

...and just some of the WEC events/ groups

Candidate Directors' Conference
International Leaders' Prayer Conference
IT Conference
Member Care Workshops
Mission and Me Weekends
Neighbours Worldwide Conference
Network Conference
Prayer Conference for WEC Retirees
Resonance Conference
Transition Seminars
UK WEC Conference
WEC Camps Reunions (Teen and Warrior)
WEC Camps Leaders' Planning
WEC France Conference
WEC Korea Board Members
WEC Short Term Leaders' Conference

photos: courtesy Kichul Jeong

above: one of the many Korean barbecues that have been prepared lovingly at Bulstrode by visiting Korean Church groups

above: a group of North Korean Christians being introduced at GOFest - most are Church or Mission leaders

The Korean Connection

Kichul Jeong

Bulstrode has always been a very special place for Korean Churches and leaders. Literally thousands of Korean pastors, Church leaders and missionaries have passed through Bulstrode during the last 20 years. Some of them were senior pastors of Mega-Churches in South Korea. And Bulstrode was the birthplace of the LMC *(London Mission Conference - annually several hundred young people gather together for world mission)* - as well as for the KMC *(Korean Missionary Council).*

GOFest Partnership

In recent years, the **GOFest** event at Bulstrode replaced WEC May Day. This annual event was larger and broader in scope, and WEC became one agency among many. A group of **Key Partners** *(Global Connections, OM, Gospel for Asia, Wycliffe Bible Translators, OMF, Gold Hill, Redcliffe College and WEC)* have worked in excellent harmony to organise the event. Local Churches like St James have supported GOFest while other Mission groups have participated with exhibitions.

The Bruderhof

David Paul

Bulstrode was purchased by the Bruderhof on 9th January, 1958 in order to have a Christian community close to London. In April 1958 some single brothers and families moved into the old mansion only to find it was riddled with dry rot. If the community hadn't worked tirelessly to eradicate it over the next 8 years Bulstrode Mansion would not still be standing. At the community's peak in 1963, Bulstrode was home to 211 brothers and sisters and children.

The community members made their living from the production of educational equipment and farm equipment under the trade names of *Community Playthings* (still in operation) and *Bromdon Products*. They also established a school and kindergarten and published Christian literature. They cleared a lot of the overgrown park and got the grounds and gardens back into condition.

On 20th March, 1966, the Bruderhof decided to close Bulstrode, and it was sold to WEC the following year. The Bruderhof was happy to find a buyer that would continue to use the property for the proclamation of the Gospel.

To the south of the Bulstrode Park there is a small burial ground containing the 18 graves of those who died at the Bulstrode Bruderhof or were buried there in the following years. It is owned, frequently visited and maintained by the Darvell Bruderhof, Robertsbridge, East Sussex.

The Bruderhof was founded in 1920 in Germany by the Protestant theologian Eberhard Arnold and his wife Emmy. Inspired by the example of the first Christians in Jerusalem, they started a community with a small group of fellow Christians in the Rhön hills. When Hitler came to power the community was under constant surveillance because of their belief in non-violence and refusal to support the Nazi Party. Soon their school was closed, their business boycotted and the young men of military age were commanded to leave the country or risk imprisonment or death.

On 14th April, 1937, secret police surrounded the Rhön Bruderhof, Germany, confiscated the property, and gave the remaining community members forty-eight hours to flee the country. By 1938, all the Bruderhof members had reassembled in England near Swindon at the Cotswold Bruderhof.

When England entered the war, the British government gave the community the option of either leaving the country as a group (including all young English members of military age) or accepting internment of all German nationals. The community, committed to staying together, decided to seek refuge abroad, where they could continue their witness of different nationalities living together in peace. They emigrated to Paraguay in South America.

Three members were left behind to settle the accounts but so many young English people wanted to join that they started a new farming community in the Clee hills of Shropshire. It was from the community in Shropshire that Bulstrode was found and purchased.

The Bruderhof Community may have left Bulstrode in 1966, but WECers living on site have had the opportunity to meet many of their members when they have returned for visits.

Many thanks to Bruderhof member David Paul for his most interesting overview and for the photos.

He adds...
there are now Bruderhof Communities in England, Germany, North and South America and Australia.
For more information please visit www.Bruderhof.com

Message from St James **Andrew Bell**

On behalf of the St James' Church leadership, Andrew writes:

Links with Bulstrode go back to the very foundation of St James' Church, Gerrards Cross in 1859 - more than 50 years before WEC was founded and more than 100 years before WEC UK came to Bulstrode. The owner of much of the land in this area was the Duke of Somerset, who rented Bulstrode House and several other properties to George Reid and his two sisters, Anna-Maria and Louisa. The Reids performed acts of charity throughout the estate, where much of the population lived in relative poverty and isolation, mostly as rural labourers. Following the death of their brother, the two sisters resolved to build a church in Gerrards Cross as a memorial. Their primary motivation, though, seems to have been their concern for the spiritual, moral and material welfare of the people.

Gerrards Cross was at the extremities of five existing parishes; the people were remote from their village centres, without the habit of church-going, and thus beyond the moral and spiritual influence of the clergy. By building St James' Church and providing for its clergymen, the sisters were already in a real sense "crossing cultures to make disciples" and "starting churches where there are few" - anticipating the current mission of WEC!

In 1967 WEC purchased Bulstrode Manor to become the Headquarters of WEC UK. Bulstrode is in St James' parish, and in the nearly half century since then, there has been a warm and synergistic relationship. St James has become the "home church" for several of the WEC team who have lived at Bulstrode, and they have been active contributors to many aspects of the life of the church. Naturally, they have helped to guide St James' mission strategy and for many years have had a presence on the Mission Committee, bringing valuable professional input to our thinking and decision-making. In addition, WEC members have contributed in many other areas; music, prayer, children's ministry and lifegroups to mention but a few.

WEC has also generously supported St James by welcoming us to Bulstrode for many church events; Alpha courses have been held there, as have committee meetings, Parish Church Council and leadership away-days. WEC has also participated in joint church activities such as 24/7 prayer and hosted, for example, joint Easter sunrise services.

In turn, St James' members have been glad to support WEC. For many years WEC, as our neighbour, has been one of our core Missions, and we have supported WEC Mission partners in prayer, practically and financially. We delight in our current relationship with the Tichy family (with WEC/Betel) in Prague. In addition, we have been able to contribute to GOFest in several ways, and individual St James' members have given their time and skills to help, for example, with accounts and budgets and in practical ways. We have also been able to host off-site strategy meetings for some of the WEC leadership.

We have valued our relationship enormously, and will continue to follow the next phase in WEC's development. We pray that God, in His wisdom and grace, will continue to use WEC in powerful ways to share Jesus where He is least known.

Worldwide Family **Christoph Lindner**

Christoph was on the St James' leadership team for 15½ years.

In 2000, Edda and I arrived in Gerrards Cross from Hamburg, Germany. We had already heard about WEC Bulstrode from friends in our church. Ever since, the people here at WEC have been a huge blessing to us - through their friendship, their example and their commitment to Christ and His mission.

We love the fact that as followers of Christ we are part of a world-wide family and the presence of WEC just around the corner has embodied that for us. So we were a little sad when the WEC International Headquarters moved to Singapore a few years ago and that WEC's time at Bulstrode is now coming to an end. At the same time we love WEC's commitment to being in the right place for *this* time to reach the nations for Christ.

When Hanni and Traugott Boeker arrived at Bulstrode they became our friends very quickly. They were for us a little bit of (German speaking!) "home from home" and have blessed us with their wisdom, resourcefulness and commitment to Christ. They have spurred us on in our own Christian journey and it's always a special treat when we manage to catch up with them.

A couple of months ago we had tea with a group of WEC "Vollies" (Volunteers). We got out a world map to find out where we are all from. We always find it inspirational to be with young people who say to God: "Here I am, Lord. Use me wherever and in whichever way You want." That is how the two of us want to live. Thank you, WEC!

St James' Church

east window, St James

Message from Gold Hill

Stephen Walker-Williams **Missional Life Pastor**

Awareness of the partnership between Gold Hill Baptist Church and WEC only goes back seven years for me; about as long as I have lived in the area. I do however remember really clearly my wife (then fiancée) first describing to me the WEC weekends with Gold Hill joining in the activities on the Sunday. To begin with I thought she was saying "WET" weekends (something that I hear on occasions it did become) rather than WEC weekends. Her face lit up as she described the setting and meeting God whilst walking and praying in the grounds. She described the sense of togetherness and excitement as hundreds of people met to worship God and learnt of his heart for the world.

For her, WEC at Bulstrode and the church joining in had been...

*a special place of encountering God
*a place of uniting friends and family
*and a place where God inspired and sent people around the world sharing Jesus

It is these three things that I now fondly associate with Bulstrode, both after hearing the memories of others from Gold Hill and also through my own experience more recently through partnership in, among other things, GOFest and supporting WEC Trek Orientation. I, like many other members of the church, have encountered God powerfully in the grounds and house of Bulstrode. We have seen God's Kingdom being built as cultural divides are broken down and people as well as Mission Agencies unite in Jesus' name and for bringing others to Him. Our partnership has made our church family richer, with greater diversity, and has supported our passion for mission.

Message from Hope

Chris Justice

Here at Hope Church, Beaconsfield *(formerly Beaconsfield Baptist Church)* we have benefited enormously, in many ways, over the years from having the WEC Headquarters so near to us. The first would be that we have had WEC missionaries and volunteers venturing over the "border" into Beaconsfield. They have brought with them their own ministries that have been great pluses to our life and mission here in the town and beyond. Secondly, those WECers have helped us to keep a much wider focus on our approach to, and involvement in, "the Great Commission"*. Thirdly, some of us have had the privilege of being involved, to a small degree, in ministering, not only to those who have been part of our congregation, but also to the wider Bulstrode community through mentoring and speaking at the morning Chapel times. *(*Jesus' words in Matthew 28:18-20)*

Another way we have benefited from being so near to Bulstrode, has been the pleasure of being part of the annual May Day event *(latterly GOFest)*. It has always been a great blessing to come and hear some inspiring speakers and, again, to have our horizons broadened by learning about God's work in other nations. And we have to say too that we have been helped and blessed by having the facilities of the building available to us for a whole variety of church meetings and events - leaders' away-days, barbecues and picnics.

For a whole host of reasons, we thank God for WEC and Bulstrode - and just as we have been the richer for having you so near, we will be the poorer when you leave the area. However, we will continue to pray for you as you begin this new chapter in your life and ministry. God bless you.

Gold Hill Baptist Church, Chalfont St Peter

the Gold Hill stand at GOFest 2015

Gold Hill Church leadership team at Bulstrode - Stephen 5th from the right

photos on this page: courtesy Joyce Gledhill, Gold Hill

A Deep and Refreshing Relationship

A Letter from Jim Graham

The Rev Jim Graham was Pastor of Gold Hill Baptist Church from 1968 to 1995.
He is 7th from the right in the picture on the previous page.

I had only been Pastor at Gold Hill Baptist Church (approximately a mile and a half from Bulstrode) for two weeks when I had a visit from Jack Aitken. He invited me to visit Bulstrode. I did this the next day and so began a relationship which brought enormous richness to my own life and to the Life of the church here.

So began a deep and refreshing relationship with some of God's very special men and women - Len and Iris Moules; Neil and Mary Rowe; Jack and Peggy Aitken; Dieter and Renate Kuhl; Robert and Isobel Mackey; Norman Grubb; Leslie and Bessie Brierley; Pak Peter Octavianus; Phil Booth and a whole multitude of others whose names still bring blessing and challenge to my life.

I was invited to join a team of the Staff Members at Bustrode as we spent a whole day praying through and "cleansing" the deep, dark basement under Bulstrode. What a day that was! What a revelation!

I used to lecture to the new Candidates on a weekly basis and they came and did outreach work into our community from the church here. What a joy to be with such dedication. Peter and Carolyn Quinton were among those Candidates but were so clearly mature and gifted. Their ministry into my life was a landmark experience to which I return again and again (no one had ever "laid hands on me" until they did).

I never encouraged WECers to join the church here because most of them had their own home churches and, anyway, their first loyalty was to the Mission and I wanted to ensure that was never compromised - yet some of them became our best "members." When Len and Iris Moules retired from the Mission they came and lived in the church's sheltered housing complex. Len became an Elder and then joined the Staff Team. What a privilege to work alongside such a man of God! Iris became a mother in God to all of us.

I profoundly thank God that during all of my "watch" as I led the church here for 27 years I had the support, backing, and encouragement of my brothers and sisters of the WEC fellowship. Their prayers lifted me and their dedication challenged me.

Bless you all, Jim

Special Occasions

Apart from external events, there are frequent occasions for fun and fellowship for the Bulstrode community itself. As you can tell from the MK Perspectives stories *(pp. 70-71)*, one of the most popular annual events is the Bulstrode Bonfire Night. The peculiar British desire to "Remember, Remember the 5th of November" can be a mystery for overseas visitors to fathom, so Lord and Lady Muddledance *(right)* or Sir William Wobblepen *(below left)* usually come along to set the historical scene.

Christmas time in more recent years has not seen the large scale concerts of days gone by, but each year in the Atrium we have still erected a spectacular Christmas tree *(pictured below)* from our faithful donor in the Missenden Valley. A Nativity Play *(pictured below right)* was performed in 2015 for the community by the Volly Helpers, and gives a glimpse of the impressive costume collection available from the WEC Youth Department. This collection, which includes hats, clothes, musical instruments and amazing artefacts from all around the world, is a tremendous resource for churches or teachers who wish to put on special cultural events. WEC Youth can also come to your church or school and help run *World Adventure Programmes.* Contact details are on the resource page *(p. 96)* at the back of the book.

photo: Crissy Brinker

photo: Rose Harvey

photo: Sam Harvey

photo: Crissy Brinker

The Ballad of the Bulstrode Boiler

Paul Harvey

Four cold months without either central heating or hot water during the winter of 2008-9 prompted Bob Dylan look-alike, Paul Harvey, to compose ***The Ballad of the Bulstrode Boiler***, sung to the tune of the 60s classic ***Bye Bye Miss American Pie*** *(Don McLean)*. The "Fab Four" performed it, and by doing so, managed to warm themselves up for a few precious moments.

The photos *(right)* show the sequence of Bulstrode boilers: the original boiler on WEC's arrival *(1967)* in what is now the Laundry Room; the next (to which the *Ballad* was dedicated) located in the Basement and bottom right, the present bio-mass boilers installed in 2014, which are fired by wood pellets.

the Fab Four - alias Brad, Paul, Moira, Sam making use of the Bulstrode Boutique's winter collection

The Ballad of the Bulstrode Boiler

Long long time ago
I can still remember
When the heating worked
and all was well;
Then the boiler broke
Everyone was freezing,
No hot water, we began to smell...

Late November made me shiver
With every email I'd deliver;
Bad news now for Bulstrode,
Everywhere was stone cold.

Second winter in a row
Icy hands and icy toes
Every type of WECer froze
the day the boiler died...

And they were singing:
"Bye, bye, Mr Boiler of old
Took my shampoo to the shower
but the shower was cold;
Them good ol' boilers had us
down on our knees, singin'
This 'll be the day that we freeze!
This'll be the day that we freeze!"

photo: WEC archives

Home Improvements over the Years

Paul Harvey

Just a few of the many improvements WEC has made to Bulstrode over the years...

top: Jean Walker clearing rubble soon after WEC had moved in

left: a new sewage system

bottom left: members of the faithful Northern Ireland team who erected the wooden stairs as well as the tractor shed

right: preparation for the new Library - seashells removed from under the floorboards were sent down a chute into a skip (p. 77)

below: Andy Pool's tea break

below right: the finished Library

below: partitions and stairs being removed to restore the Verandah Lounge to its original shape and size

photo: Richard Davey

central six photos: Richard Davey

The Farewell Coffee

The morning coffee/tea break is a time when Bulstrode personnel tend to come together - so it has always been a good moment to bid farewell to any who are leaving.

The photo to the right shows John Bagg *(UK Director)* wishing farewell to Chuck and Cathy Odegaard, who were Bulstrode Managers 2014-15.

PART FIVE

A NEW SEASON

The Goodbye Wave

And in the time-honoured tradition of goodbyes at the porch of Bulstrode, the gathered family *(below)* waved a fond farewell to Derryck and Tineke Orridge as they departed at the end of January, 2016. No, not to the heart of Africa, but to Yorkshire. This was one of the last porch gatherings, with everyone else getting ready to leave later in the year. For the *final* final farewell, it would be nice for *all of us* to wave *all of us* off at the porch, but apart from being logistically challenging, it could waste a lot of packing time.

A New Season for WEC in the UK

Relocating away from Bulstrode represents a radical shift in thinking, and heralds a "new season" for WEC International in the UK. The four boxes below, gleaned from presentations given by the UK leadership in the spring of 2016, summarise (i) the changing nature of mission in today's society (ii) WEC UK's response to this (iii) new strategic directions for ministry and (iv) how individuals, both present WECers and new recruits, can become involved in this exciting new adventure with God.

(i) What trends do we see affecting the UK?

*Increased secularisation, pluralism and postmodern spiritualism

*Unprecedented migration bringing both opportunities for witness and enrichment to the UK Church

*Decline of the Western Church, the demise of Christendom and the marginalisation of Christianity

*Decline in vision for the overseas "unreached" therefore decreased resources/recruitment

*Increased cultural diversity meaning the gospel needs fresh interpretations and communication

*Evolving role of traditional Mission Agencies and their relationship to the local church and the established denominations

*Growth of the church in the global South and the development of WEC International in Asia and Africa

(ii) How is WEC responding?

***WEC UK – is reordering for renewal and fruitfulness**

*WEC UK's desire is ***to be a growing, fruitful, vibrant movement of Christ worshippers committed to working together, with the UK Church and the worldwide fellowship of WEC***

*To fulfil this we are reordering, redistributing resources and decentralising to form clusters of workers around the country - a critical mass of like-minded people working together to reflect the values, and further the objectives of WEC International.

*Though this means many changes, WEC UK remains true to its core vision statement: ***"To see Christ known, loved and worshipped amongst the unreached peoples of the world."***

(iii) Strategic Direction

*Go into communities **out there** and live amongst the people

*Form clusters of workers in key geographic areas (especially urban) in order to make new contacts, develop relationships, and **grow our influence** across the nation

*Foster **relationships** with local churches, in order to seek out fresh links and networks

*Develop our national presence by **serving and equipping** individuals and local churches for cross-cultural ministry

*Maintain a **prophetic voice** - continue to be advocates for unreached peoples

*Establish ministry hubs to better **serve our people**

(iv) How can I engage with this vision?

***The strands of ministry that can give you some initial pointers:**

Engage	Disciple	Mobilise
Recruit	Support	Prayer

***Current ministries that can provide you with an opening:**

Neighbours Worldwide	Resonance Arts
Geared for Growth	Youth/Camps
WEC Short-Term	Publications
Radio Worldwide	Mobilising

Our support structures, based in a more focussed HQ, include:

Leadership	Communications
Operations	Member Care and Personnel

Or...have you got a vision to start something different?

Appendix 1 - Picture Gallery

some final glimpses of the mansion and grounds

Atrium landing

Laundry ceiling

Garden Room - many a Candidate interview took place here

Laundry - many a sock was washed here

worn down step to the Laundry - 150 years' footfall

"The Son of Man did not come to be served, but to serve, and to give His life as a ransom for many." (Mark 10:45)

arch into the Stable Wing

below: vapour trails above the neighbouring horse field, illustrating that Bulstrode lies under the flight path for Heathrow

above: arch to the Stables Wing - drawing by Charlton Smith

below: dappled sunlight through the Tulip Tree

the neighbouring horse field, used by Pinewood Studios for movies such as Charlie and the Chocolate Factory and Maleficent

300 year-old Cedar of Lebanon by the Long Water

Handkerchief Tree

Wisteria

a host of golden Daffodils

view from the south

"Going home" - two-toned, stormy sky behind Bulstrode hill

"Morning has broken" - view from the editor's flat

Snowy Bulstrode

flooding - a third lake for Bulstrode

photo: Anthony Lau

view from the northwest

Appendix 2 - Contacts and Resources

WEC International

www.wec-uk.org
office@wec-uk.org
facebook.com/WECUK
twitter.com/wecuk
instagram.com/wecuk
issuu.com/wecuk

WEC Publications

www.worldmissionsbooks.com
wecbooks.blogspot.co.uk
@wecmissionbooks
www.smashwords.com *(search here for 19 WEC e-books incl. "Why on Earth a Mansion?")*

WEC Youth and WEC Camps

www.weccamps
youth@wecinternational.org.uk
(contact here for info regarding World Adventure Programmes and more resources)

Resonance Arts Ministry

www.resonancearts.net
resonance@wecinternational.org
facebook: ResonanceArts
twitter: ResArtsUK

For other WEC ministries (Geared for Growth, Neighbours Worldwide, Radio Worldwide, Betel etc) contact WEC International

Books about Bulstrode

Baker, Audrey & Edmonds, GC	**A History of Chalfont St Peter and Gerrards Cross/The History of Bulstrode** (2003, Colin Smythe Ltd)
Hunt, Julian & Thorpe, David	**Gerrards Cross, A History** (2006, Phillimore & Co Ltd)
Bakewell, Gillian & Reynolds, Peter	**Bulstrode: its History in Articles from the Internet** (2009, WEC)

Books by WECers or about WEC and mission

Bardsley, John	**He Gives Us Authority** (2012, WEC Publications)
Bearup, Colin	**Keys: Unlocking the Gospel for Muslims** (2009, WEC Publications)
Burnett, David	**World of the Spirits** (2000, Monarch Books) plus **The Spirit of China** and other titles
Chevreau, Guy	**We Dance Because We Cannot Fly** (2008, 1st Harper Collins, 2nd Sovereign World)
Davies, Evan	**Beyond the Edge: 100 Stories of Trusting God** (2012, CLC Publications)
Davies, Evan	**Whatever Happened to CT Studd's Mission?** (2012, WEC Publications)
Dinnen, Stewart	**How Are You Doing?** (2001, Christian Focus Publications)
Dwight, Mike	**Out of the Desert** (2015, New Wine Press) also **Into the Land**
Gaynor, Lily & Butterworth, John	**God's Needle** (2012, Monarch Books/Lion Hudson)
Grubb, Norman	**CT Studd: Cricketer and Pioneer** (1933, reprint 2012, Lutterworth Press)
Johnstone, Patrick	**The Future of the Global Church** (2011, Authentic Media Ltd, Biblica in the USA)
Kallmier, Jen	**The Golden Chariot** (2012, Christian Focus Publications)
Kilbourn, Phyllis	**Children in Crisis** (1996, World Vision Resources) plus **Street Children** and other titles
Lidorio, Ronaldo	**Unafraid of the Sacred Forest** (2007, Christian Focus Publications)
McElligott, Patrick	**On Giants' Shoulders** (1991, 2004, WEC Publications)
Myers, Glenn	**More Than Bananas** (2014, Fizz Books)
Operation World (Mandryk, Jason)	**Operation World** (2010, InterVarsity Press)
Operation World (Wall, Molly)	**Pray for the World** (2015, InterVarsity Press)
Parkes, Trudi	**40 Days 40 Bites** (2014, Christian Focus Publications)
Ross-Watson, Michael	**Climbing Higher Daily Readings** (2015, available from Amazon)
Spraggett, Daphne & Johnstone, Jill	**Window on the World** (2001, Angus Hudson Ltd, Paternoster in the USA)
Sutton, Susan	**Designer Living** (2014, CLC Publications) and other titles
Tepper, Elliott	**The Cost of the Kingdom** (2012, Amistad Comunicaciones; 2013, Christian Focus Publ.)
Vincent, Eileen	**No Sacrifice Too Great** (1992, WEC Publications)

Some other titles

Baker, Rob	**Adventures in Music and Culture** (2012, Ambassador Books)
Hunt, Ulrike	**Yeshua Unlocked** (2012, www.lulu.com) plus other titles
Verwer, George	**Drops from a Leaking Tap** (2009, Authentic UK) plus **More Drops** and other titles

Music resources

Baker, Adam	**Your Eyes** **Beyond the Sun**	(www.adambakermusic.co.uk)
Harvey, Paul M	**Story Songs from the Book of Faith** **Remember Your Creator**	(paulmh247@gmail.com, bible100s.co.uk)
Latin, Lorraine	**Hope in You**	(www.hopeinyoualbum.com)